Apache Open Office 3.4: Using Base

JAMES STEINBERG

ISBN: 149279399X
ISBN-13: 978-1492793991

DEDICATION

To Zizzi and Harry, thanks for all your support

.

CONTENTS

ACKNOWLEDGMENTS

I would like to express my very great appreciation to the OpenOffice.org team and volunteer community for all their efforts in furthering the development of the Apache Open Office application.

Additional thanks to Ian Mugridge for the time that he spent collecting and formatting the images used in this book.

1.   INTRODUCING OPENOFFICE.ORG

1.1   What is OpenOffice.org

OpenOffice.org is a productivity suite, which is provided as a freely available open source product. The software is maintained and developed by a community of volunteers. This book was written based on version 3.4.1 of the OpenOffice.org suite, which was the latest version at the time of writing.

The OpenOffice.org suite includes the following applications –

1.1.1   Writer

Writer is OpenOffice.org's word processing tool that enables the easy creation of books, reports, letters and other documents. Writer documents can have objects from other open office tools inserted into them and the documents can be exported in a number of formats such as HTML, PDF and Microsoft Word.

1.1.2   Calc

Calc is OpenOffice.org's spreadsheet program. It has advanced features chart generation and over 300 financial, mathematical and statistical functions. Calc can open Microsoft Excel documents and also export to them, as well as PDF and HTML formats.

1.1.3   Impress

Impress is OpenOffice.org's presentation tool, which can incorporate the graphics capabilities of the Draw and Math programs. Impress can open Microsoft PowerPoint files and save files in a number of formats.

1.1.4   Draw

Draw is OpenOffice.org's drawing tool, which can be used to produce anything from simple flowcharts to complex 3D artwork. Draw can import and export a number of formats such as JPG, PNG and PDF.

1.1.5   Base

Base is OpenOffice.org's database component. It provides all the expected functions of a database frontend such as reports, queries, forms and views. It can connect to a number of different database engines such as Access, MySQL, Oracle and any ODBC or JDBC compliant databases.

1.1.6   Math

Math is OpenOffice.org's equation and formula editor. It allows the user to create complex equations using symbols not available in standard font sets. The output from Math can be inserted into other OpenOffice.org documents, but can also be saved in the Mathematical Mark-up Language format for use in other documents.

1.2   Advantages of OpenOffice.org

There are a number of advantages of OpenOffice.org over other office suites, such as -

- The software is open source and has no licensing fees - you are free to distribute, modify and copy the software as much as you like, subject to the OpenOffice.org Open Source license.
- The software is cross-platform, running under multiple operating systems such as Windows, OS X and Linux.
- Support for multiple languages, in both the user interface and spelling/thesaurus facilities.
- The user interface is consistent between the individual applications in the suite.
- Support for a number of different file formats, including PDF, Microsoft Office, XML, HTML, Word Perfect and Lotus 1-2-3.

1.3   System requirements

OpenOffice.org 3.4 runs on a number of different operating systems, such as -

- Microsoft Windows 2003, XP, Vista, 7 and 8.
- GNU/Linux kernel version 2.6 and glibc 2.11.1 or higher.
- Mac OS X 10.4 or higher.

Hardware wise, the requirements depend on the operating system, but can be broadly summarised as follows –

- 256Mb of RAM (512Mb recommended – on Mac OS 512Mb is required).
- 400Mb of available disk space (on Windows 650Mb is required for the installation process, but temporary install files will be deleted afterwards).
- 1024 x 768 or higher screen resolution with at least 256 colours (Mac OS requires 16.7 million colours).

Some of the features of OpenOffice.org require the Java Runtime Environment 1.5.x or higher to be installed on the computer. However, OpenOffice.org will run without JRE being installed, there will just be some features such as wizards that will not be available.

1.4   Obtaining the software

As mentioned above, OpenOffice.org is open source and has no licensing fees. The latest version can be downloaded from the OpenOffice.org website. The installation package is fairly large, so if you have a slow Internet connection, you may prefer to purchase a copy on a CD/DVD from a third-party distributor. There is a list of distributors on the support website (http://distribution.openoffice.org/cdrom/sellers.html), but remember that the distributors are not endorsed by OpenOffice.org.

1.5   Installing the software

You can download a detailed guide on installing OpenOffice.org from http://wiki.services.openoffice.org/wiki/Documentation, and the basics can be found from http://download.openoffice.org/common/instructions.html.

1.6   Add-ons and extensions

There are many extensions and add-ons available to enhance OpenOffice.org, which are available from the official extensions repository - http://extensions.services.openoffice.org/. Many are free, but some are charged for.

1.7   Starting OpenOffice.org

There are a number of different ways of starting OpenOffice.org and the applications that make up the suite.

1.   Use the Start menu (on Windows - it will be called the Application menu if you are using Mac OS X) and select OpenOffice.org from the OpenOffice.org folder - this will start the OpenOffice.org Start Centre, from where you can create individual documents.
2.   Use the Start menu (or equivalent) and select the application (i.e. Writer or Calc) that you want to run.
3.   Start from an existing document. If you already have a Writer or Calc document that you want to open then you can double click on that document to open the corresponding application.
4.   If you are using Windows, you can use the Quickstarter, which is described below.
5.   You can also start OpenOffice.org using your operating system's command line.

1.7.1 Using the Windows Quickstarter

The OpenOffice.org Quickstarter is an icon in the Windows system tray that indicates that OpenOffice.org has been loaded and is ready for use. To open a new OpenOffice.org document using the Quickstarter, right-click on the icon to open a pop-up menu (Figure 1). You can then start a blank document of a particular type or use "Open Document" to open the documents folder and select a document.

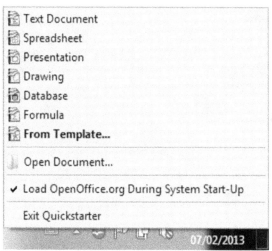

Figure 1: Quickstarter pop-up menu

1.7.2 Disabling Quickstarter

If you want to stop OpenOffice.org from loading during start-up (for example, if your computer has insufficient memory), then deselect the **Load OpenOffice.org-dev During System Start-up** option on the pop-up menu.

1.7.3 Re-enabling Quickstarter

If you have disabled the Quickstarter and want to re-enable it, select the **Load OpenOffice.org during system start-up** checkbox in **Tools > Options > OpenOffice.org > Memory**.

1.7.4 Using the command line

You can load OpenOffice.org from the command line, which will give you more control over what happens when it starts. For example, you can tell Calc to load a document and then print it. To just start Math with a blank document you can use the option:

soffice -base

You can start other OpenOffice.org components using the following command line options -

Type of document	Command line option
Text	-writer
Spreadsheet	-calc
Drawing	-draw
Presentation	-impress
Formula	-math
Database	-base
Web page	-web (opens using Writer)

You can see a list of the options available when starting OpenOffice.org using the **soffice -?** option, which will return something like **Figure 2**.

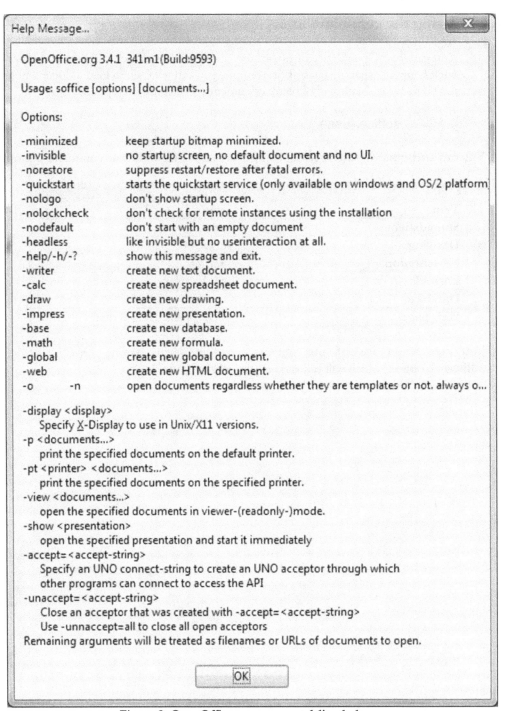

Figure 2: OpenOffice.org command-line help

1.8 The OpenOffice.org GUI

The main window of OpenOffice.org contains a number of features that are common across the different components of the package. These common features include the menu bar, the formatting toolbar, the standard toolbar and the status bar at the bottom of the application window.

The individual chapters on the components detail the features that differ between the components.

1.8.1 Menu bar

Each component has a Menu bar at the top of the window, below the Title bar. The menu bar will allow you to access a number of functions available for the specific component. The menu bar has the options listed below and selecting a menu option will result in a submenu being displayed that shows the commands available.

- File is the option used for working with commands that apply to the whole document such as opening and saving.
- Edit contains commands for editing the document, such as copying and pasting parts of the document.
- View is used for controlling the display of the document, such as specifying the zoom level to be used.
- Insert allows you to insert elements such as pictures, headers and footers into your document.
- Format is used for the commands that provide formatting to your document, such as Styles.
- Table holds the commands for working with tables in a text document.
- Tools has the commands for performing Spelling and Grammar checks.
- Window contains the commands that are used for the display window.
- Help provides links to the OpenOffice.org Help file and other help/information commands.

1.8.2 Toolbars

Below the Menu bar are a number of toolbars, some of which are common across all the components of OpenOffice.org, whilst others are dependent on the component being run.

The first common toolbar is the Standard toolbar, which contains the commands for opening, saving, printing, spellchecking etc. The second common toolbar is the Formatting toolbar, which is context-sensitive. This toolbar will change depending on the document element that is currently selected. For example, if the cursor is in text, the toolbar will display the commands for formatting text.

1.8.3   Displaying or hiding toolbars

You can decide which toolbars are displayed by using the **View > Toolbars** menu option. Use the checkboxes to indicate which toolbars are to be displayed.

1.8.4   Toolbar types

OpenOffice.org had three different types of toolbar: floating, docked and tear-off. Docked toolbars are attached to the toolbar area, but can be moved positions within that area and can also be made to float. Floating toolbars appear over the main document editing area and can be docked if required. Tear-off toolbars are additional toolbars that appear as options from another toolbar icon.

1.8.5   Tear-off toolbars

Tear-off toolbars are selected from toolbar icons that have a small triangle to the right. Clicking on the triangle will display the tear-off toolbar. As the name suggests, the tear-off toolbar can be torn off from its parent icon and either left floating or docked along an edge. Figure 3 shows an example of a tear-off toolbar.

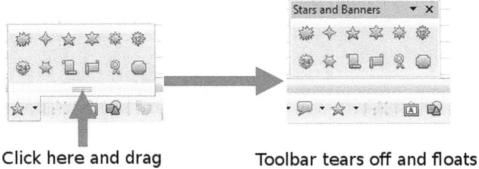

Click here and drag   Toolbar tears off and floats

Figure 3: Tear-off toolbar

1.8.6 Moving toolbars

Both docked and floating toolbars can be moved. Docked toolbars have a small vertical bar on the left of the toolbar (the toolbar handle - see Figure 4), put the mouse pointer over this and hold down the left mouse button and drag the toolbar to the new location.

Handles of docked toolbars

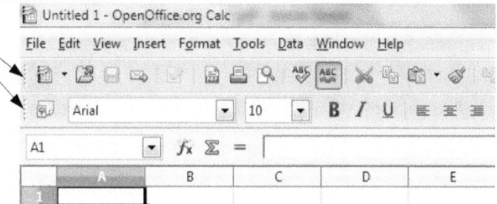

Figure 4: Moving a docked toolbar

Floating toolbars are moved by clicking on the title bar and dragging it to the new location (Figure 5).

Title bar of floating toolbar

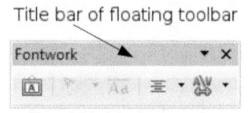

Figure 5: Moving a floating toolbar

1.8.7 Docking/floating toolbars

To dock a currently floating toolbar, hold down the Control key and double-click on the frame of the floating toolbar and this will dock it in its last position.

To float a docked toolbar, hold down the Control key and double-click on the frame of the docked toolbar.

1.8.8 Customising toolbars

There are several ways that toolbars can be customised, such as locking the position of a docked toolbar and choosing which icons are shown. The customisation options are accessed using the down-arrow on the toolbar's title bar or at the right-hand end of the toolbar (depending on whether it is floating or docked).

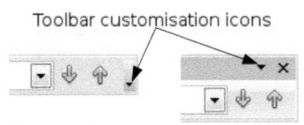

Figure 6: Toolbar customisation

The **Visible buttons** option on the drop-down menu that is shown will allow you to select the icons to be shown (visible icons have an outline around them) and the Lock Toolbar Position will lock a docked toolbar.

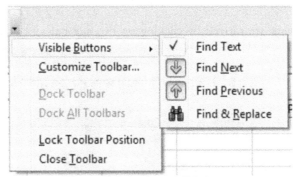

Figure 7: Selecting visible icons

1.8.9 Context menus

Many of the menu functions can be accessed by right-clicking on a document element such as a paragraph or an image. This will result in a context menu popping up.

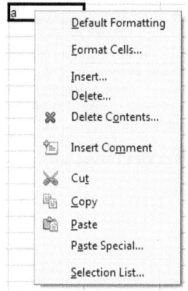

Figure 8: Context menu for a cell in Calc

1.8.10 Status bar

At the bottom of the workspace is the Status bar, which provides information about the document. The layout of the Status bar is common between the different components of OpenOffice.org, although there are some specific items for each component.

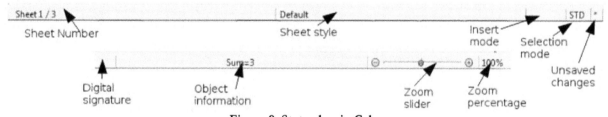

Figure 9: Status bar in Calc

The common status bar items are -

- **Page, sheet or slide number** - shows the current page, sheet or slide number and the total number of slides. Double-clicking on this brings up the Navigator.
- **Page style** - shows the current style or slide design. Double-clicking on this allows you to edit the current style.
- **Unsaved changes** - If changes to a document have not been saved, an asterisk (*) appears here.
- **Digital signature** - If the document has been digitally signed, an icon will appear here. Double-clicking on the icon will display the certificate.
- **Object information** - Displays information relating to the cursor's position or the selected element of the document. Double-clicking will open the relevant dialog.
- **Zoom slider and percent** - Allows you to change the magnification by dragging the slider or clicking on the + and - signs. Double-clicking on the Zoom percent area opens the **Zoom & View Layout** dialog.

1.9   Starting a new document

When OpenOffice.org is open, but no document is loaded, the Start Centre is shown. You can click on one of the icons to open a blank document of that type or use the Open option to open an existing document or the Templates option to start a new document using a particular template.

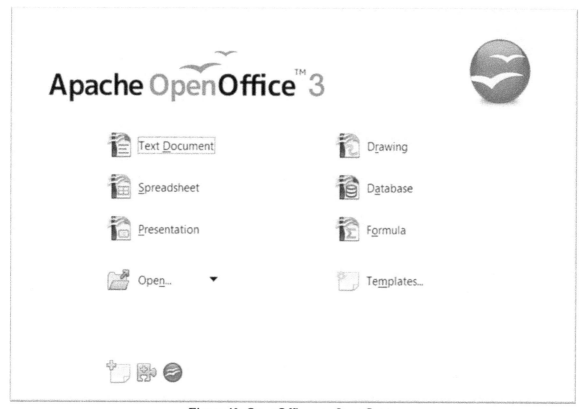

Figure 10: OpenOffice.org Start Centre

You can also start a new document in the following ways -

- Press *Control+N* on the keyboard.
- Use the arrow next to the **New** button on the main toolbar and select the type of document from the drop-down menu.
- Use **File > New** and chose the type of document.
- Use **File > Wizards** for special types of document such as a letter or a Web Page.

1.10 Opening an existing document

As mentioned in the section above, the Start Centre has an icon for opening existing documents, which will also allow you to access a list of recently edited documents.

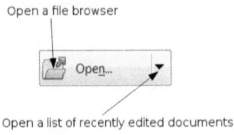

Figure 11: Start Centre existing documents icon

You can also open existing documents in the following ways -

- Press *Control+O* on the keyboard.
- Use the **Open** button on the main toolbar.
- Use **File > Open**.

Regardless of which approach you use, the Open dialog will appear allowing you to select the required document and click **Open**.

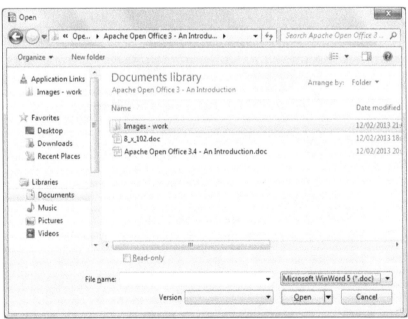

Figure 12: Open dialog

It is also possible to open a document directly from Windows Explorer by double-clicking on the file.

1.11 Saving a document

To save an existing document with the same file name, use **File > Save** or use the **Save** button on the main toolbar. This will overwrite the existing file.

To save a new document for the first time, you can do one of the following:

- Press *Control+S* on the keyboard.
- Use the **Save** button on the main toolbar.
- Use **File > Save**.

This will open the Save As dialog, where the file name can be entered and **Save** pressed to save the file.

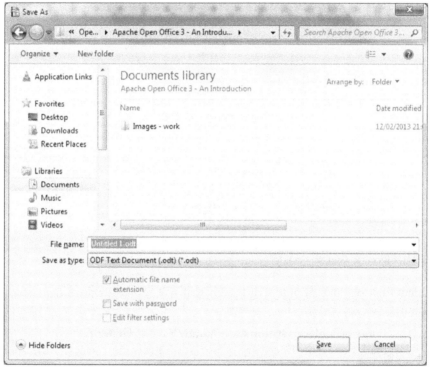

Figure 13: Save dialog

1.11.1 Password Protection

It is possible during the save process to protect the document so that it cannot be opened without a password. On the Save As dialog, select the **Save with password** option and click **Save** and you will open the Set Password dialogue, where you can enter the password you wish to use.

Figure 14: Set password dialogue

OpenOffice.org uses a very strong encryption mechanism that makes it virtually impossible to recover the document contents should you forget the password.

1.11.2 Autosaving documents

OpenOffice.org has an autosave option that will save your document automatically every X minutes. To set up automatic saving:

1. Choose **Tools > Options... > Load/Save > General**.
2. Mark **Save AutoRecovery information every**, and select a time interval.

1.12 Using the Navigator

The Navigator shows objects within a document, grouped into categories. For example, in Writer it will show Headings, Text Frames, Tables, Bookmarks etc.

The Navigator can be opened by pressing *F5*, clicking its icon ⊘ on the Standard toolbar or by **View > Navigator** on the menu bar.

Figure 15: The Navigator

If you click the plus sign to the left of the category, it will expand to display the list of objects in that category. You can use the Navigator to move around the objects within a document, by double-clicking on an object to jump directly to that object's location.

You can jump to a specific page in the document, by typing its page number in the box at the top of the Navigator.

You can also use the Navigation icon  to display the Navigation toolbar, which allows you to select a category using the icons and then use the Next and Previous icons to move from object to object.

Figure 16: Navigation toolbar

1.13 Undo and Redo

You can undo the most recent change, by pressing *Control+Z*, clicking the **Undo** icon  or using **Edit > Undo** on the menu bar. The Edit menu will show what change is going to be undone.

Figure 17: Edit > Undo menu item

If you use the Undo icon, then clicking the triangle to the right of it will list all of the changes that can be undone and it is possible to select multiple changes and undo them at the same time.

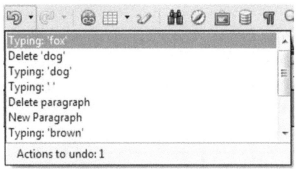

Figure 18: List of changes that can be undone

Once you have undone some changes, **Redo** becomes active allowing you to redo a change. To do this, you can press *Control+Y*, click the **Redo** icon or select **File > Redo**. If you use the icon, you can use the triangle to the right to get a list of changes that can be redone.

It is also possible to change the number of changes that OpenOffice.org remember, by choosing **Options > OpenOffice.org > Memory** and in the Undo section change **Number of steps**.

1.14 Closing a document

You can close a document by using the **File > Close** menu option or by clicking on the **Close** icon in the document window. If the document has not been saved since the last change then a message box is displayed asking if you want to save changes. The message box gives three choices:

- **Save** - The document is saved and then closed.
- **Discard** - The document is closed and the changes since the last save are lost.
- **Cancel** - The close option is cancelled and you are returned to the document.

> Not saving your document could result in the loss of recent changes or even worse, your entire document.

1.15 Differences between operating systems

Some of the keystrokes and menu items are different on a Mac than those used in Windows and Linux. The table below shows some of the common differences. A more detailed list can be found in the application Help.

Table 1: Differences between operating systems

Windows/Linux	Mac equivalent	Effect
Tools > Options menu selection	OpenOffice.org > Preferences	Access setup options
Right-click	Control+click	Open context menu
Ctrl (Control)	⌘ (*Command*)	Used with other keys
F5	Shift+⌘+F5	Open the Navigator
F11	⌘+*T*	Open the Styles and Formatting window

James Steinberg

2 INTRODUCING BASE

2.1 What is Base?

Base is OpenOffice.org's database program, which allows the storage of pieces of information that are in some way related to each other. In this book, I will give details of how to create a database, how to create forms and reports and also how to register external data sources within Base.

2.2 The Base interface

When you first start Base, the **Database Wizard** will be shown, which will allow you to either open an existing database or create a new one. This is described in section 5.1.

Once you have completed the database wizard, the main Base window will be opened, as shown in **Figure 19**.

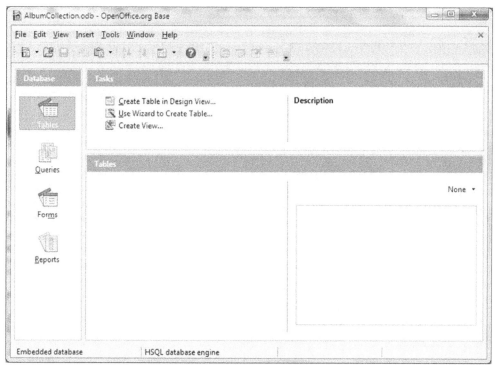

Figure 19: Base window

The window is split into six sections. The menu bar, toolbar and status bar are described in Chapter **Error! Bookmark not defined.**, the remaining three sections are described below.

2.2.1 Database section

The **Database** section allows you to select which of the four types of elements of the database you want to work with. You can choose from:

- **Tables**
- **Queries**
- **Forms**
- **Reports**

These elements are all detailed in subsequent chapters.

2.2.2 Tasks section

The **Tasks** section changes depending on which element is selected and displays tasks that apply to the selected element. These are normally tasks such as creating elements.

2.2.3 Elements section

This section changes its name depending on the type of element that is selected and displays a list of all of the elements of that type in the database. Hence when Tables is selected all of the tables will be listed here. Double-clicking on an element will open it.

3   SETTING UP BASE

3.1   Options affecting all of OpenOffice.org

There are options that can be changed that affect all of the components of OpenOffice.org. This chapter will concentrate on those options that are important when using Base. The other general options are described in *Apache OpenOffice.org 3.4: An* Introduction.

Select the **Tools > Options** entry on the menu bar and the Options – OpenOffice.org dialog will open. The list in the left-hand box show the individual options that can be changed – the content of the list varies based on which component of OpenOffice.org is open. Click the marker next to OpenOffie.org to display all of the suite-wide options that are available. Selecting an item will cause the relevant page to be displayed in the right-hand side of the dialog.

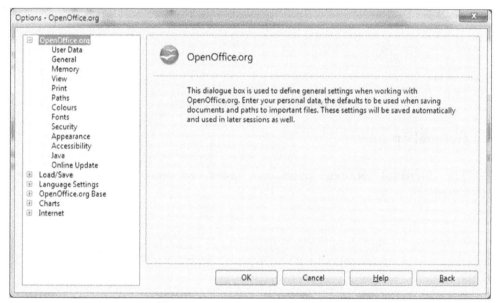

Figure 20: OpenOffice.org options

3.1.1 User Data options

The information stored in the **User Data** page is used in a number of places within Writer, such as in the document properties to record who the document was created by and last edited by and also the name of the author for changes and comments. To change these details, fill in or update the form that is displayed.

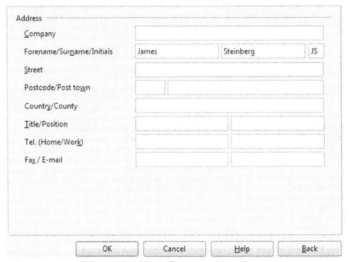

Figure 21: User Data options form

3.1.2 General options

The **General** options page has some general options about the setup of OpenOffice.org.

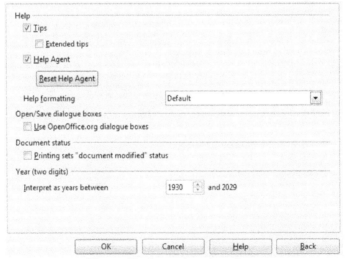

Figure 22: General options form

- **Help – Tips** – If *Tips* is selected, then when the mouse pointer is over an icon, one or two words will appear.
- **Help – Extended Tips** – When *Extended Tips* is selected, a short description of the function of a particular menu command or icon will be shown when the mouse pointer is over that item.
- **Help – Help Agent** – The *Help Agent* is similar to Microsoft's Office Assistant. To turn it off, deselect the option and to restore the default behaviour, click **Reset Help Agent**.
- **Help – Help Formatting** – This area changes the system colour scheme to improve readability. You can chose from a number of high contrast styles:

High-contrast style	Visual effect
Default	Black text on white background
High Contrast #1	Yellow text on black background
High Contrast #2	Green text on black background
High Contrast Black	White text on black background
High Contrast White	Black text on white background

- **Open/Save Dialogs** – You can chose to use your operating system's standard Open and Save dialogs instead of the OpenOffice.org dialogs. To use the operating system dialogs, deselect the **Use OpenOffice.org dialogs** option.
- **Document Status** – If you select the **Printing sets "document modified" status** option then the next time you close the document after printing, the print date will be recorded in the document properties as a change. This will result in you being asked to save the document, even if you have made no other changes.
- **Year (two digits)** – This option defines how two-digit years are interpreted. For example, if you set the two-digit year to 1935, then entering a date of 1/1/35 or later will result in the date being interpreted as 1/1/1935 or later. A value "below" 1/1/35 is interpreted as the following century; i.e. 1/1/29 would be interpreted as 1/1/2029.

3.1.3 Memory options

This page controls how OpenOffice.org uses your computer's memory and the amount of memory it requires. It is important to consider though that there is a trade-off between allocating more memory to OpenOffice.org to speed it up and reducing the amount of memory available to other applications.

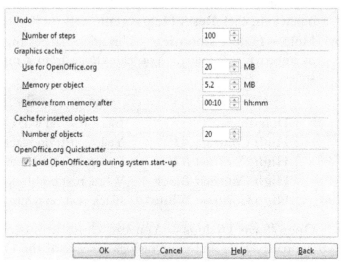

Figure 23: Memory options

3.1.4 View options

The **View** options page change the way that the document window looks and acts.

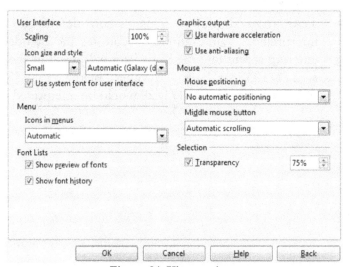

Figure 24: View options

- **User Interface – Scaling** – You can change the size of the text in help files or on menus by changing the scaling. Increasing the factor will increase the size of the text.
- **User Interface – Icon Size and style** – You can use the two options her to change the size of the icons in the toolbar and also the style/theme of icons used.
- **User Interface – Use system font for user interface** – Selecting this option uses the system font rather than OpenOffice.org's provided font for the user interface.
- **Menu – icons in menus** – This option causes icons to be displayed in the menus.
- **Font Lists – Show preview of fonts** – If this is selected, the font list displays the font name using the individual font.

Figure 25: Font list examples, without preview (left) and with (right)

- **Font Lists – Show font history** – Selecting this causes the last five fonts you have used in the current document to be displayed at the top of the font list.
- **Graphics Output – Use hardware acceleration** – Selecting this option means that OpenOffice.org directly accesses the hardware features of the graphic display adaptor to improve the screen display.
- **Graphics Output – Use anti-aliasing** - Disables and enables anti-aliasing, which smooths the edges of graphical objects and improves the look of them.
- **Mouse – Mouse positioning** – Allows you to specify where the mouse pointer will be positioned when a dialog is opened.
- **Mouse – Middle mouse button** – Defines what action occurs when the middle mouse button is pressed.
- **Selection – Transparency** – Defines the appearance of selected text with a shaded background. Increase or decrease the Transparency setting to make the background more or less dark. Deselecting the option results in the selected text appearing in reversed colour.

3.1.5 Print options

The Print options page allows you to set your printing to match your default printer.

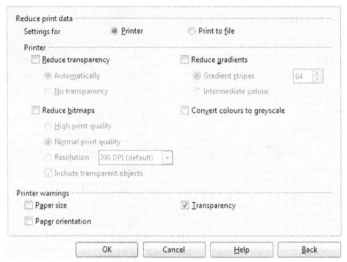

Figure 26: Print options

The *Printer warnings* section allows you to select whether you want to be warned if the paper size or orientation in the document does not match the settings available on your printer.

3.1.6 Paths options

The **Paths** options page allows you to change the location of files used by OpenOffice.org.

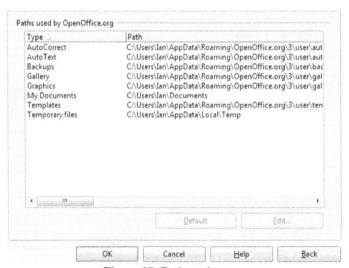

Figure 27: Path options

To change a path, select an item in the list and click **Edit**, which will display the Select Path dialog, where you can select the path required for the specific item.

3.1.7 Colours options

The **Colours** options page allows you to specify the colours to be used in OpenOffice.org documents. You can select colours from the colour table, edit existing colours or define new ones.

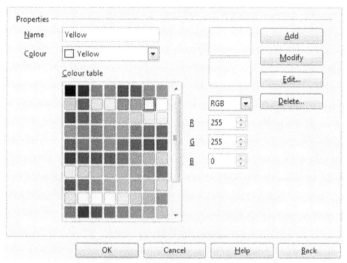

Figure 28: Colours options

If you want to edit a colour, you can use the **Edit** button to open the Colour Picker dialog (**Figure 29**), where you have a much greater deal of control over the choice of colour, such as using RGB, CMYK or HSB values.

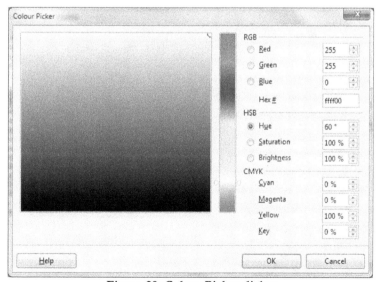

Figure 29: Colour Picker dialog

3.1.8 Fonts options

The **Fonts** options page allows you to specify the replacements for any fonts that appear in a document, but are not installed on your system. OpenOffice.org has a default that it will substitute for fonts that it does not find, but this page will allow you to specify a different one than is used as standard.

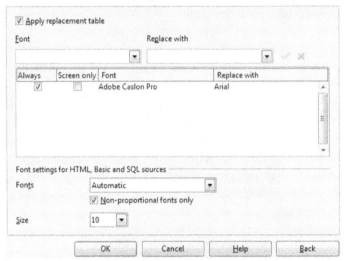

Figure 30: Font options

The bottom section of the page allows you to change the typeface and size used for displaying source code such as HTML and SQL.

3.1.9 Security options

The **Security** options page allows you to select the security options for loading and saving documents:

Figure 31: Security options

The top section of the page allows you to select when you want to receive warnings about hidden information, or have it removed on saving. The bottom of the page deals with Macro security.

Pressing the **Options** button will display the **Security options and warnings** dialog:

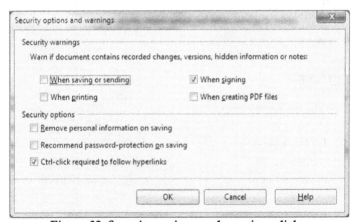

Figure 32: Security options and warnings dialog

The first section of this dialog allows you to specify when you should be warned about hidden information and notes etc., whilst the bottom of the dialog allows you to specify if personal information should be removed on saving and how hyperlinks are treated.

If you press the **Macro security** button the **Macro Security** dialog opens:

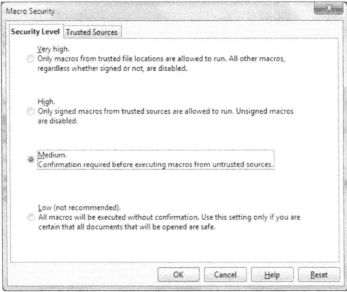

Figure 33: Macro Security dialog

In the Macro Security dialog, you can adjust the security level for executing macros.

3.1.10 Appearance options

The **Appearance** options page allows you to specify the layout formatting option that are displayed, and the colour they are displayed in. This includes items such as page breaks, section breaks and boundaries of tables and objects:

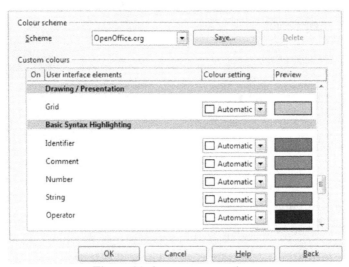

Figure 34: Appearance options

To show or hide an item, select or deselect the checkbox next to the item's name. Some items, such as Document background, are mandatory and cannot be deselected. To change the default colour of an item, click the down-arrow in the *Colour setting* column and select the new colour.

3.1.11 Accessibility options

The **Accessibility** options page allows you to specify options that affect the accessibility of the applications for users with a visual disability.

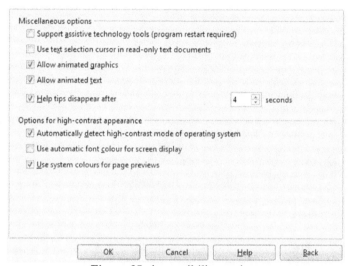

Figure 35: Accessibility options

3.1.12 Java options

The **Java** options page allows you to select the Java Runtime Environment (JRE) to use and set parameters relating to it.

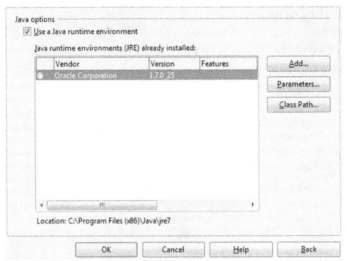

Figure 36: Java options

3.1.13 Online Update options

The **Online Update** options page allows you to select how often OpenOffice.org checks for updates and whether they are automatically downloaded.

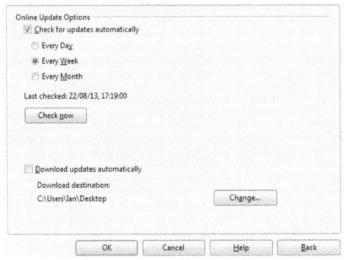

Figure 37: Online Update options

3.2 Load and Save options

OpenOffice.org provides the facilities to set the Load and Save options as best suits the way you work. This is done using the **Load/Save** option of the Options dialog. Click on the symbol to the left of **Load/Save** to expand the options choices.

3.2.1 Load/Save – General options

The **General** options page allows general load and save related settings such as AutoRecovery and default file formats to be updated:

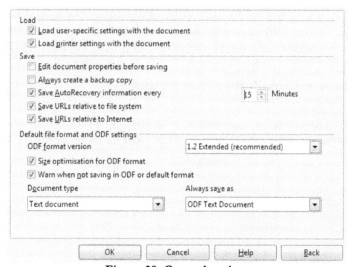

Figure 38: General options

- **Load user-specific settings with the document** – This setting allows you to specify whether your settings (such as printer name) are overwritten by the settings used by the person who saved the file.
- **Load printer settings with the document** – If this is **not** selected, then the printer details saved with the document will be ignored and the default printer in your system will be used.
- **Edit document properties before saving** – If this setting is selected then the **Document Properties** dialog will pop-up for information to be entered the first time you save a new document or use **Save As**.
- **Save AutoRecovery information every** – Setting this option turns on the automatic saving of recovery information every X minutes, allowing you to retrieve a recent copy of the document if there is some sort of system failure.
- **Save URLs relative to file system** and **internet** – These two options set the addressing of documents relative to the directory where the current document is stored.
- **Default file format and ODF settings** –
  - o **ODF format version** – By default, OpenOffice.org saves documents in

35

the latest OpenDocument Format (ODF version 1.2 Extended). If you are sharing documents with people who are using older versions of OpenOffice.org, then you can change this setting to save the document using ODF version 1.0/1.1.

o **Size optimization for ODF format** – OpenOffice.org documents are saved as XML files and can be viewed as such using a text editor. However, the files are optimised to reduce space by not storing the indents and line breaks. Deselecting this option will result in the indents and line breaks being stored, so that the document is easier to read in a text editor.

o **Document type** – This section will allow you to specify the file format that is used to save individual OpenOffice.org files. For example, if you regularly share spreadsheets with Microsoft Office users, you might want to set Calc to save the documents in one of the Microsoft .xls formats.

3.2.2 Load/Save – VBA Properties options

OpenOffice.org can load and save Microsoft Office document formats and any VBA code that is included with them. This option page specifies how the VBA code is handled.

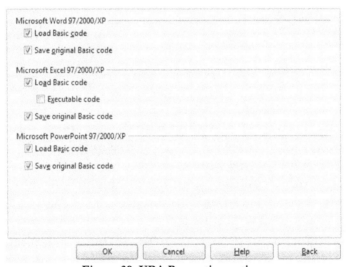

Figure 39: VBA Properties options

If you choose **Load Basic code to edit**, then the code is available for editing, but the changed code will not be retained if you save in a Microsoft Office format. Choosing **Save original Basic code** will result in the macros being commented out in OpenOffice.org format, but retained if the file is saved in Microsoft Office format.

3.2.3 Load/Save – Microsoft Office options

OpenOffice.org can load and save documents in Microsoft Office formats and this page allows you to specify how linked or embedded objects (OLE) are handled. Selecting the [L] option will result in the Microsoft OLE objects being converted to the corresponding OpenOffice.org OLE object when a Microsoft document is loaded. Selecting the [S] option will result in any OpenOffice.org OLE objects being converted into the corresponding Microsoft OLE objects, when a document is saved in a Microsoft format.

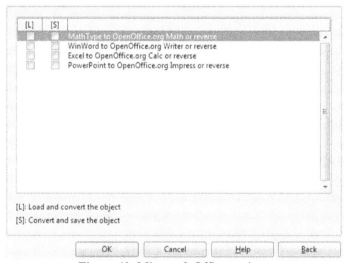

Figure 40: Microsoft Office options

3.2.4 Load/Save – HTML Compatibility options

This options page allows you to set how HTML pages are imported and exported with OpenOffice.org.

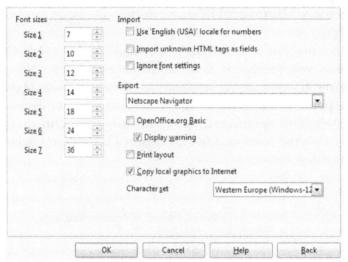

Figure 41: HTML Compatibility options

- **Font sizes** – This setting allows you to specify the respective font sizes for the HTML <font size=x> tags.
- **Import – Use 'English (USA)' locale for numbers** – this setting allows you to control the decimals and thousands characters that are used when importing numbers in an HTML page. If this setting is selected, then the English (USA) locale will be used, otherwise OpenOffice.org will use the locale setting defined in OpenOffice.org (see page 39).
- **Import – Import unknown HTML tags as fields** – If this setting is selected then any tags that are not recognised by OpenOffice.org will be imported as fields. Opening tags will have an HTML_ON field created and closing tags an HTML_OFF field. When the document is exported as HTML, the fields will be converted to tags.
- **Import – Ignore font settings** – This setting will make OpenOffice.org ignore internal font settings and use the fonts that were specified in the HTML Page Style instead.
- **Export** – This setting allows you to specify a browser or HTML standard in the drop-down selection, and exported files will be saved to meet that setting.
- **Export – OpenOffice.org Basic** – If you select this setting then OpenOffice.org Basic macros will be saved as part of the header of the HTML document. This option must be selected *before* the macro is created, otherwise the script will not be inserted.

- **Export – Print layout** – Selecting this option will enable the exporting of the print layout of the document.
- **Export – Copy local graphics to Internet** – If this option is selected then any embedded pictures will be automatically uploaded to the Internet server when the document is uploaded using FTP.
- **Export – Character set** – This option allows you to select the character set for the export.

3.3 Language Settings options

Within OpenOffice.org, you can change the languages that are used in both the user interface and as a default for documents. This is done using the **Language Settings** pages of the **Options** dialog.

If you want to work with a language other than those of the dictionaries that are automatically installed with OpenOffice.org, then you will need to use the **Tools > Language > More Dictionaries Online** option to install the additional languages that you require.

3.3.1 Language Settings - Languages options

This page allows you to update the locale and language settings that OpenOffice.org uses for the user interface, locale, currency and documents as required.

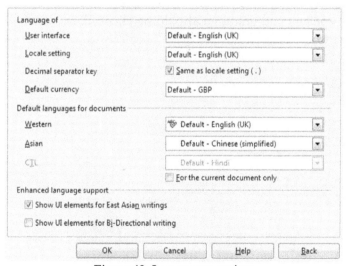

Figure 42: Languages options

If you wish to use Asian (Chinese, Japanese, Korean) languages or CTL (Complex Text Layout) languages such as Urdu or Hebrew then you can select the additional options. If you select one of these options then the next time you open this dialog, you will see extra choices under **Language Settings**.

3.3.2 Language Settings – Writing Aids options

The Writing Aids options page allows you to specify the options for checking spelling and grammar.

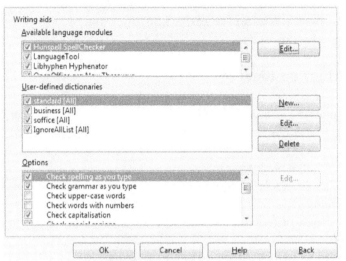

Figure 43: Writing Aids options

You can use the **New, Edit** and **Delete** options in the **User-defined dictionaries** section to work with additional dictionaries and also choose whether modules such as the Thesaurus should be used. Additionally, you can use the **Options** section to specify if spelling and grammar should be checked as you type and whether to check uppercase words etc.

3.4   Base specific options

The OpenOffice.org Base section of the Options dialog allows you to set options that are specific to Base.

3.4.1   Connections

The **Connections** page of the options allows you to set how the connections to data sources are pooled.

The Connections facility allows you to stipulate that connections that are no longer needed are not deleted immediately, but are kept free for a certain period of time. If a new connection to the data source is needed in that period, the free connection can be used for this purpose.

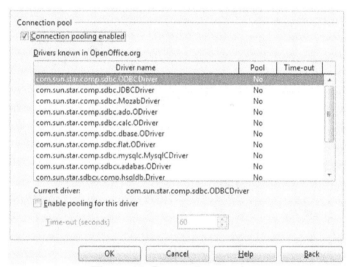

Figure 44: Connections options

3.4.2 Databases

The **Databases** page of the options add, modify, or remove entries to the list of registered databases. You must register a database within OpenOffice.org in order to see it in the View - Data sources window.

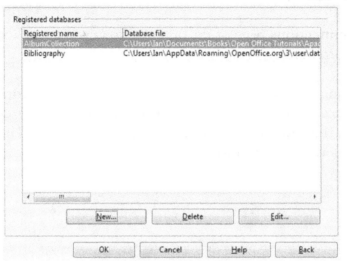

Figure 45: Databases options

3.5 Chart options

3.5.1 Default Colours options

The **Default Colours** page of the options allows you to set the colours that are used for each of the data series in the charts.

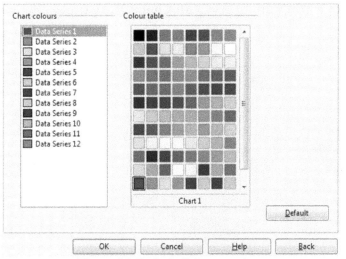

Figure 46: Default Colours options

3.6   Internet options

The **Internet** options pages allow you to set up how OpenOffice.org works with the Internet.

3.6.1   Proxy options

The **Proxy** page of the options allows you to set up options relating to proxy servers that you want to use with OpenOffice.org.

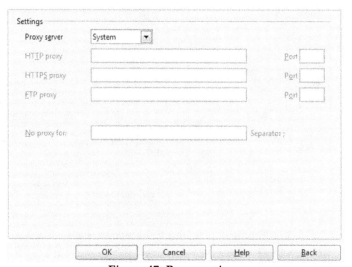

Figure 47: Proxy options

3.6.2 Search options

The **Search** page of the options allows you to set up the search engine settings that are used with OpenOffice.org.

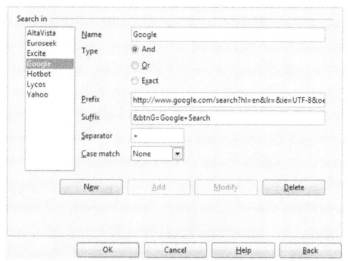

Figure 48: Search options

James Steinberg

4 INTRODUCING DATABASES

4.1 Introduction

There are different types of databases, the discussion of which is beyond the scope of this book, all you need to know is that Base creates a *relational database*. In a relational database, the stored information is spilt up into *tables*, which contain *fields*. Each table will contain a number of *records*.

Simple Album database example

Consider a database that has been designed to hold the details of a collection of Albums. The information that you might want to hold could include the name of the Album, the year that it was released and the name of the artist or group that recorded the Album.

We could store all of this information into a single table within the database and have a record relating to each Album, storing its name, the name of the artist and the year it was released. This would be fine if an artist only ever recorded one Album, but it can be seen; from the snippet of the table below; that as an artist is likely to record a number of Albums over their career, we will be storing a lot of duplicate information.

AlbumName	Artist	Released
The Clash	The Clash	1977
Give 'Em Enough Rope	The Clash	1978
London Calling	The Clash	1979
In The City	The Jam	1977
This is the Modern World	The Jam	1977

4.1.1 Relationships

Taking our example above, it can be seen that there is a relationship between the CD name and the Artist, relationships can take three different forms:

- *One-to-one relationship.* An example of a one-to-one relationship is a person and a national insurance number. Only one person can have a particular national insurance number, and a national insurance number can only belong to one person. Where there is a one-to-one relationship, the data will normally be stored in one table, so for example national insurance number would just become a field on the person table.

- *One-to-many relationship.* An example of a one-to-many relationship is an employee/department relationship. An employee will have one department and a department will have many employees. Where there is a one-to-many relationship, it is usual to have two tables with link between them at the one end, so each department would have an id and the employee would have a department id field.

- *Many-to-many relationship.* An example of a many-to-many relationship is a student/lesson relationship. A student will have many lessons and a lesson will have many students. To implement a many-to-many relationship, it is necessary to have three tables, the two required tables and a linking table. This in effect breaks down the many-to-many relationship into two one-to-many relationships. So, we would have a student table, a lesson table and student_lesson table. The student_lesson table would just hold the identities of the student and the lesson concerned.

Improved Album database example

If we look at the Album database example given previously, we can see that there is a one-to-many relationship between Albums and Artists. We can therefor split our database into two linked tables – Albums and Artists.

AlbumId	AlbumName	ArtistId	Released
1	The Clash	1	1977
2	Give 'Em Enough Rope	1	1978
3	London Calling	1	1979
4	In the City	2	1977
5	This is the Modern World	2	1977

ArtistId	ArtistName
1	The Clash
2	The Jam

The Album table will now hold an ArtistId, rather than the artist's name. This Id links to a field on the Artists table, enabling us to display the artist responsible for a particular album, as will be seen later in the book.

The above might seem like a lot of effort to go to for little apparent gain, but if you consider that a commercial database may store many millions of records then the space saving between storing an id number as opposed to a repeated name, which could be up to 40 or 50 characters is massive.

4.1.2 Keys

For a database to be useful, it is necessary to be able to uniquely identify an individual record. If you look at our example Albums database, you would rightly say that the Album Name is a unique identifier (based on the records shown). However, consider a CD called "The Greatest Hits", I am sure that there will be many artists who have issued a CD with that name, so we would have to use the Album Name and Artist Id to identify a particular CD. Then consider that an Artist could conceivably issue two CDs of the same name at different times, so do we have to add Released into the unique identifier as well? Things will soon start to get complicated, but there is an alternative solution. You might have noticed the AlbumId field that has mysteriously appeared in the CDs table and appears to serve no purpose. It is in fact providing a unique identifier to each record in the Albums table. Such a field is known as a *primary key* and the Artist Id field on the Albums table is known as a *foreign key*.

4.1.3 Forms

Within Base, you can define a *form*, which will allow you to enter data into the fields of one or more tables. You can also use *queries* to build a temporary table from the contents of existing tables and then use a *report* to present the results of a query in the desired format.

4.1.4 Queries

Queries provide the power behind a database, by writing a query, you can display the contents of a table (or multiple tables) in a different format, as shown by the two examples below.

Querying our Album database examples

Queries provide a powerful way of presenting the information in a database to meet specific requirements. Base provides a number of graphical ways for generating queries, but for the purpose of these examples, we will use the raw SQL (Structured Query Language) that actually does the work behind the scenes. It should be noted that there are a number of different varieties of SQL, so the one used below may not work on a different database system.

Limiting the results

Let's assume that you want to see just the names of all the albums that were released in 1977, in alphabetical order. Our query would be:

SELECT AlbumName FROM Album WHERE Released = 1977 ORDER BY AlbumName ASC;

And the resulting table returned would be

AlbumName
In the City
The Clash
This is the Modern World

Composite results

Looking at just our Album table, it is difficult to know who recorded a particular Album as all we have to go on is an ArtistId. With a query though we can produce a temporary table that tells us everything about an Album:

SELECT AlbumName, ArtistName, Released FROM Album, Artist WHERE Album.ArtistId = Artist.ArtistId ORDER BY ArtistName ASC, Released ASC

This would give us the following table

AlbumName	ArtistName	Released
The Clash	The Clash	1977
Give 'Em Enough Rope	The Clash	1978
London Calling	The Clash	1979
In The City	The Jam	1977
This is the Modern World	The Jam	1977

SQL queries are very powerful and the above are fairly simple examples. Chapter 10 provides more details of the syntax of SQL and some more complex examples.

4.1.5   Views

A *view* is a virtual table, which is created dynamically when access to that table is required. A view can be comprised of one or more tables and is based on a query.

The advantage of a view is that it can be used as part of a query, to simplify the overall query.

4.2   Planning a database

The first step in designing a database is planning it and analysing what your requirements for the database are. You can do this by asking yourself questions about the information you want to be able to store.

For the purpose of the rest of this chapter, we will use an expanded version of our Album database that will be used to store not only the Album and artist, but also individual tracks on an Album and the format (CD, vinyl, cassette etc) that the Album is owned in.

The book will walk you through the creation of the database, but if you want to download a complete version, you can download it from my website. You can find it at http://www.jamessteinberg.info/open_office_introduction_files.php.

From this brief description, we can see that there are four individual tables that would be useful in our database:

- Album
- Artist
- Format
- Track

We now need to consider the relationships between the tables and will assume the following:

- An Artist can record many Albums.
- An Album can only be recorded by one Artist (we will ignore collaborations).
- An Album can have many tracks on it.
- A track can only appear on one Album (it will be treated as a different track on other albums).
- An Album is only owned in one Format
- Multiple Albums of a particular Format can be owned.

Now that we have a broad idea of the tables that we need, it is time to consider the information that we want to store about each Artist, Album, Format and Track. This can be as simple or as complex as you require, but for the purpose of our example, we will keep it fairly simple and store the following information:

- Album – title, released year, cover photo
- Artist – name, formation year, disbanded year
- Format - name
- Track – name, length

We will also add Id fields to each of the tables to use as a primary key. Additionally, to enable linking between the tables, they will need foreign keys.

We now have a logical model for our database, which we will now convert in to the physical database using Base.

5   CREATING A NEW DATABASE

5.1   The Database Wizard

When you first start Base, the **Database Wizard** will be shown, which will allow you to either open an existing database or create a new one. On the first page of the **Database Wizard**, select **Create a new database** and click **Next**.

Figure 49: Database Wizard page 1

On the second page of the wizard, there are two questions. Select **Yes, register the database for me** and **Open the database for editing** and then click **Finish**.

Figure 50: Database Wizard page 2

 By registering the database, we make it available to other OpenOffice.org components such as Calc. If it is not registered then they will not be able to access it.

Save the new database with the name *AlbumCollection*, and the database window will open.

6 CREATING TABLES

6.1   Introduction

At present, we have an empty database file, so it is time to start building our database by adding in tables. Click the *Tables* icon in the *Database* list or press *Alt+A* to select table mode and the *Tasks* list will update to display the tasks that can be performed on a table and the existing tables will be displayed in the *Tables* area.

The Tasks list displays the following options:
- Use Wizard to Create Table
- Create Table in Design View
- Create View

6.2   Using the Table wizard

Base provides a wizard to simplify the process of creating tables, by providing a selection of pre-defined table structures, which you can alter if necessary to meet your needs. One of the tables offered by the wizard is a CD-Collection table, which we will use as the basis of our Album table.

6.2.1   Step 1: Selecting fields

Click **Use Wizard to Create Table** to open the **Table Wizard**.

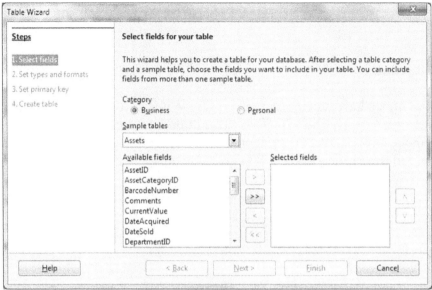

Figure 51: Table Wizard page 1

We can now select the fields that we want for our Album table:

- The wizard categorises tables as either Business or Personal, in this case the CD-Collection table is categorised as Personal, so select Personal.

- Select CD-Collection from the **Sample tables** drop-down and the available fields updates to show the CD-Collection table's fields.

- There are a number of fields on this sample table, but we do not need all of them. Individually select the CollectionID, AlbumTitle, Format and ReleaseYear fields (in order) in the **Available fields** list and press the **>** button after selecting each one.

- We are left with one field that we haven't created – the cover photo. Fortunately, you can add fields from multiple tables to your new table, so click on the Business category and select the Employees table. You can now add the Photo field to our selected fields in the same way as before.

- Click the **Next** button

6.2.2 Step 2: Setting field properties

You should now be on page 2 of the Table Wizard, which will enable you to set properties for each of the fields.

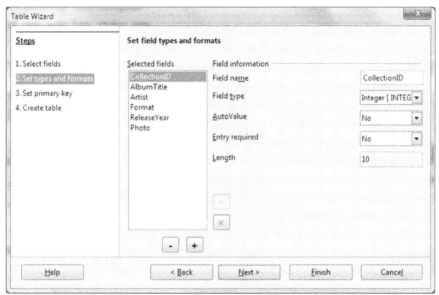

Figure 52: Table Wizard page 2

Select each of the fields in order and make the following changes to the default values:

- CollectionID
  - ○ Change Field name to **AlbumID.**
  - ○ Change AutoValue to **Yes.**
- AlbumTitle
  - ○ Change Entry required to **Yes**.
- Artist
  - ○ Change Field type to **Integer**.
  - ○ Change Entry required to **Yes**.
- Format
  - ○ Change Field type to **Integer**.
  - ○ Change Entry required to **Yes**.
- ReleaseYear – use the default settings.
- Photo – use the default settings.

Click the **Next** button.

6.2.3   Step 3: Defining the primary key

You should now be on page 3 of the Table Wizard, which will enable you to set the primary key (the unique identifier) for the table.

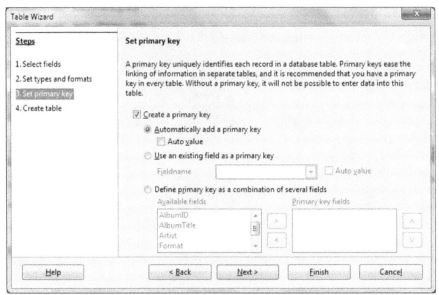

Figure 53: Table Wizard page 3

1. Ensure that Create a primary key is selected.
2. Select the Use an existing field as a primary key option.
3. Select AlbumID from the Fieldname dropdown list.
4. Ensure that Auto value is selected.
5. Click **Next**

6.2.4 Step 4: Creating the table

You should now be on page 4 of the Table Wizard, where we actually create the table.

Figure 54: Table Wizard page 4

1. Rename the table to Album.
2. Click **Finish** to create the table and then close the window that opens.

You will now be back at the main database window and you will see an entry named "Album" in the Tables area of the window.

6.3   Using Design View

Design View provides a more advanced means of creating a new table, by directly entering the information about each field in the table. We will use Design View to create the Artist table for our database. First of all, click **Create Table in Design View** to open the Design View window.

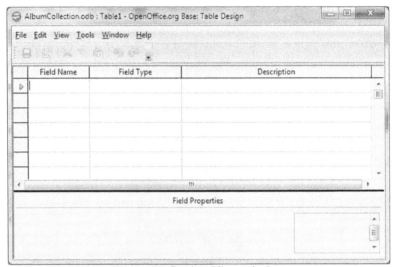

Figure 55: Design View window

We will now enter each field in order:

1. ArtistID
   a. Type *ArtistID* in the first Field Name and press *Tab* to move to the Field Type column.
   b. Select *Integer [INTEGER]* as the Field Type from the dropdown list.
   c. In the Field Properties section at the bottom, change *AutoValue* to *Yes*.
   d. Right-click on the green triangle to the left of *ArtistID* and choose *Primary Key* from the menu.
2. ArtistName
   a. Type *ArtistName* in the Field Name.
   b. In the Field Properties section, increase the Length to 100.
3. FormationYear
   a. Type *FormationYear* in the Field Name.
   b. Change the Field Type to *Integer [INTEGER]*
4. DisbandedYear
   a. Type *DisbandedYear* in the Field Name.
   b. Change the Field Type to *Integer [INTEGER]*

You do not need to put anything in *Description*, but can if you want to provide yourself with details of what the field is used for. Once you have completed the above, select **File > Save** and name the table *Artist* and then close the Artist table.

We have now walked through setting up two of our four tables, the rest will be the same, so take some time now to set up the *Format* and, *Track* tables. Remember to add an ID field where required to use as a primary key. Also, consider the suitable format and lengths for your fields (for example Format.Name will probably not need to be 100 characters long and there is a Time format that you could use for the Track.Length).

You should now have a database with four empty unrelated tables.

6.4   Copying an existing table

If you have a number of tables that have the same structure, then rather than creating each table from scratch you can create one table then make copies of it:

1. Right-click on the table you want to copy and select **Copy** from the context menu.
2. Move the mouse pointer to below the table and right-click and select **Paste** to open the **Copy Table** dialog.

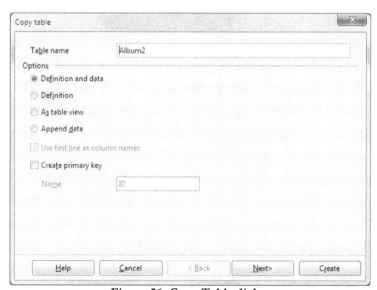

Figure 56: Copy Table dialog

3. Change the name of the table and press **Next**
4. Click the **>>** button to move all the fields from the left box to the right box and press **Next**.

5. Make any changes that you require to the Field Types.
6. Click **Create**.

6.5 Editing tables

If you want to edit a table's structure after you have created it, right-click on the table name and select **Edit** this will open the table in Design View. You can then edit field properties and add and delete fields.

6.6 Creating views

First of all, click **Create View** to open the **View Design** screen. This screen look and works like the **Query Design** screen that is described in section 9.3.

It is only sensible to create views after you have defined the relationships between your tables, otherwise the views will not work as you expect.

7 RELATIONSHIPS

7.1 Defining the relationships

We identified the relationships between our tables when we were planning our database. You will recall that we had a number of 1-to-many (1:n) relationships.

Now, we will define those relationships in Base. Open the **Relation Design** window by choosing the **Tools > Relationships** menu option. You will see that the **Add Tables** dialog is also opened.

Figure 57: Relation Design window and Add Tables dialog

You can add tables by either double-clicking on them or selecting them and pressing **Add**. Do this for all of the tables and then click **Close** to close the dialog.

The tables will have been added to the **Relation Design** window all in a row in the order you added them. Drag them around until they look like the figure below.

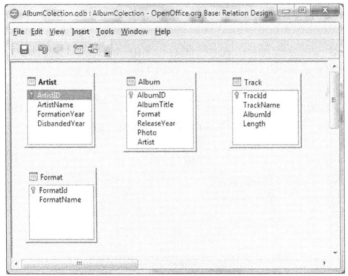

Figure 58: Relation Design window

There are two different ways of defining the relationship between two tables:

- Drag the linking field from one table to another.

- Use the **New Relation** icon to open the **Relations** dialog.

7.1.1 Dragging to define relations

Drag the *ArtistID* field from the *Artist* table to the *Artist* field on the *Album* table and release the mouse button. This will add a line with the relationship between the two tables.

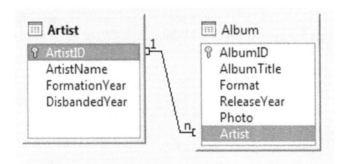

Figure 59: 1:n Relationship

7.1.2   Using the Relations dialog

Pressing the **New Relation** icon will open the **Relations** dialog.

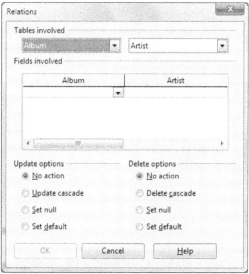

Figure 60: Relations window

Ensure that the *Album* and *Track* tables are selected in the **Tables involved** section. Then select the *AlbumID* in the **Fields involved** section and press **OK**.

The **Update options** and **Delete options** sections determine how records are updated and deleted when records in a related table are updated or deleted. For example if we consider the *Album* and *Track* tables, which are related using the *AlbumID* field. If we delete a record from the *Album* table, this will leave records in the *Track* table that are no longer related to an album. This can be handled in four ways using the options on the dialog:

- **No action** – no action is taken and the ID field in the *Track* table will still contain the id of the deleted album. This leads to orphaned records.
- **Delete cascade** – when an *Album* record is deleted, all the records in *Track* with that *AlbumID* are also deleted.
- **Set null** – the *AlbumID* field in the *Track* table are set to Null.
- **Set default** – the *AlbumID* field in the *Track* table are set to a previously defined default value.

65

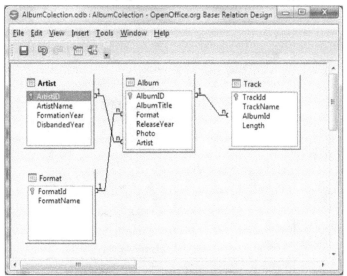

Use either of the above two methods to add a relationship between the *Album* and *Format* tables and you should end up with something that looks like the below.

Figure 61: Complete relationship design

Save and close the window to return to the main Base window. We now have four empty tables that have relationships.

8   FORMS AND DATA ENTRY

8.1   Directly entering data

We will see in Section 8.2 how to build forms for the entry of data, but sometimes that is not necessary. Take for example the *Format* table. This will be a small table with just a few entries in it – in the time it takes to build a form, we could have typed the data in to the table directly.

Double-click on the *Format* table to open the **Table Data View** window.

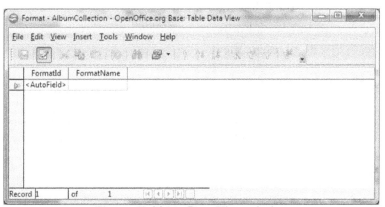

Figure 62: Table Data View window

You will see that there are two column headings matching our field names and an area below for the actual data. Because the table is currently empty all you will see is <AutoField> in the *FormatId* field.

Click in the *FormatName* field and type "Cassette Tape" and press **Enter**. You will see that the *FormatId* field changes to 0 and a new empty row is added. Do the same for CD and Vinyl (and any other formats you want to use). You will see that the *FormatId* increments for each record that we add.

We could use this method for entering all the data into our database, but it would be time-consuming and you would also have to remember what each Id represented.

8.2   Creating forms

We now need a way of getting the remaining data into our database. We could just open the **Table Data View** and enter the data directly into the table (we saw this for the *Format* table), but this is not really user-friendly. To improve the entry of data, Base allows you to design forms that will present the user with the data entry requirements.

Click the *Tables* icon in the *Database* list or press *Alt+A* to select table mode and the *Tasks* list will update to display the tasks that can be performed on a table and the existing tables will be displayed in the *Tables* area.

The Tasks list displays the following options:
- Use Wizard to Create Form
- Create Form in Design View

8.3   Using the Form wizard to create a simple form

We will start by creating a simple form that will be used to add a new Artist to the database. This form will just collect the information that is required in the *Artist* table.

8.3.1   Step 1 – Select Fields

Click on the **Forms** icon in the left-hand column and then select **Use Wizard to Create Form** to open the first page of the **Form Wizard**.

Figure 63: Form Wizard page 1

Under **Tables or queries** select **Table: Artist** and the list of fields will update to show the fields in the *Artist* table.

Select the *ArtistName*, *FormationYear* and *DisbandedYear* fields and press the **>** button to add them to the **Fields in Form** section. We do not need to add *ArtistId* as it will be auto-updated and doesn't need a value entered.

Press the **Next** button twice.

8.3.2 Step 2 – Arranging the controls

You will now be on page 5 of the **Form Wizard**.

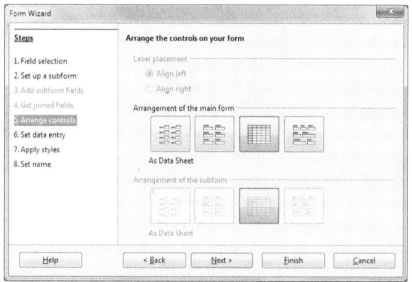

Figure 64: Form Wizard page 5

On this page you can choose the way that the Controls and their labels are placed on the form. Choose the first icon (**Columnar – Labels Left**) and press the **Next** button.

8.3.3   Step 3 – Setting data entry

You will now be on page 6 of the **Form Wizard**.

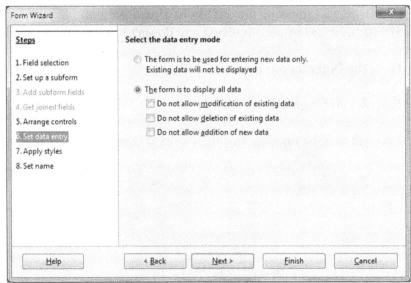

Figure 65: Form Wizard page 6

This page allows you to select how the form interacts with existing and new data. Our form will be used to view and update existing data as well as adding new records, so just leave the settings as they are and press the **Next** button.

8.3.4 Step 4 – Selecting a style

You will now be on page 7 of the **Form Wizard**.

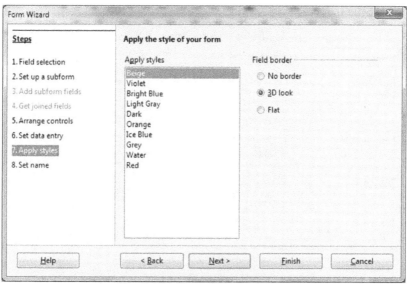

Figure 66: Form Wizard page 7

This page allows you to modify the colour and border styles of the form. Play around with them until you find a combination you like (changes will update in the form behind).

When you are finished press the **Next** button.

8.3.5 Step 5 – Setting the name

You will now be on page 8 of the **Form Wizard**, where you can set the name of the Form.

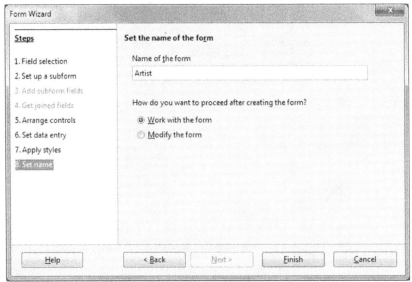

Figure 67: Form Wizard page 8

Change the name of the form to "Artist Entry" and press **Finish**.

The form wizard will close and the **Database Form** window will open showing the form ready for you to enter some data.

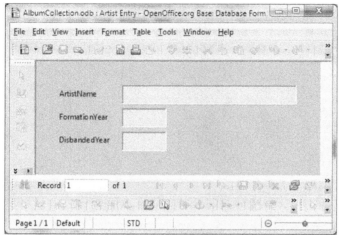

Figure 68: Database Form window

Below the main form are some controls, which are ghosted out at the moment.

Enter the details of a couple of your favourite bands (it doesn't matter if you don't know when they were formed or disbanded as you can leave those fields blank).

At least some of the controls at the bottom should now be active:

Figure 69: Database Form window controls

From left to right, the controls are:
- **Find Record** – allows you to search for a particular record.
- **Absolute Record** and **Total No. of Records**. You can enter a value in Absolute Record to jump to that record.
- **First Record**
- **Previous Record**
- **Next Record**
- **Last Record**
- **New Record** – jumps to a blank record.
- **Save Record**
- **Undo: Data Entry**
- **Delete Record**

When you have finished entering Artists, close the **Database Form** window and double click on the *Artists* table in the main Base window.

You should see something that looks like the below.

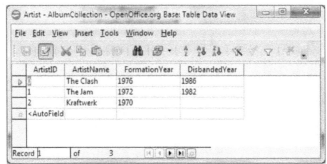

Figure 70: The Artist table

You will see that even though we didn't enter an *ArtistId*, one has been allocated to each of the records.

8.4 Using the Form wizard to create a form with subforms

We could create a form for each of our tables/queries and just enter the data for each *Album* and *Track* individually, but Base will allow us to simplify the process by defining a form with a subform using the Form Wizard.

Start up the Form Wizard as before.

8.4.1 Step 1 – Select fields

The main table for our form will be the *Album* table, so select that in the **Tables or queries** section and then select all of the fields except *AlbumID* and then press the **Next** button.

8.4.2   Step 2 – Setting up a subform

You should now be on page 2 of the Form Wizard.

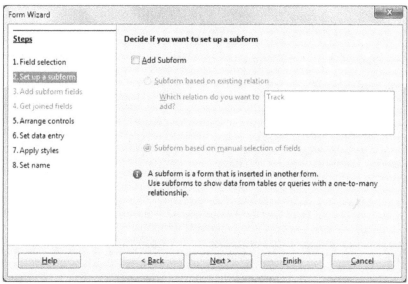

Figure 71: Form Wizard page 2

Select the **Add Subform** option and then ensure that the **Subform based on existing relation** option is selected, and select the *Track* relation. Then press the **Next** button.

8.4.3   Step 3 – Adding subform fields

You should now be on page 3 of the Form Wizard.

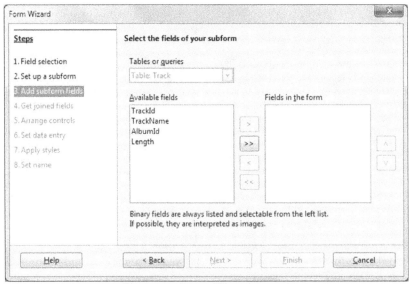

Figure 72: Form Wizard page 3

We need to add fields from the *Track* table, which is already selected, so add the *TrackName* and *Length* fields. Then press the **Next** button.

8.4.4   Step 4 – Arranging the controls

This step is the same as with the simple form built earlier, except that you can choose different arrangements for the form and subform. For the main form, select the **Columnar – Labels Left** icon and leave the subform as **Data Sheet**. Then press **Next**.

8.4.5   Step 5 – Set data entry

You can leave the default values here and just press **Next**.

8.4.6   Step 6 – Apply styles

Set the style up so that it matches your other form and press **Next**.

8.4.7   Step 7 – Set name

Change the name to "Album and Tracks" and press **Finish**.

You should now be presented with a form that looks something like the below.

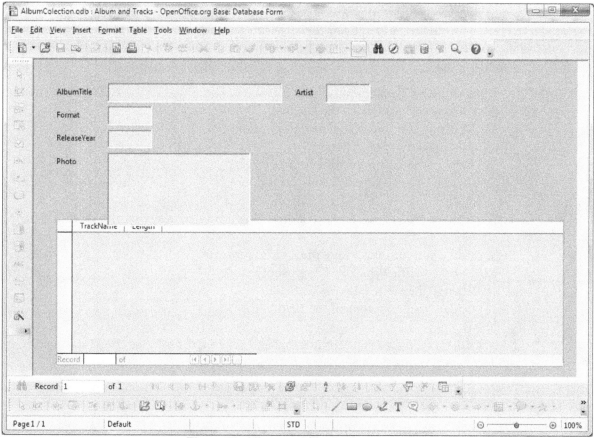

Figure 73: Album and Tracks form

The form is not quite ready for entering data just yet though. You will see that the fields are not well arranged and that the *Artist* and *Format* fields are currently set as text fields that could take any value. To ensure the integrity of the database, we need to ensure that these can only be set to values that are in the *Artist* and *Format* tables respectively.

8.5   Modifying the form

Once you have produced your initial form with the **Form Wizard,** you can modify it to fix any problems, add in drop-down selections and change the background etc.

For our *Album and Tracks* form, we will make the following changes:

1. Change the background of the form.
2. Change the colours of the labels.
3. Rearrange the fields so that they are tidier
4. Add a heading for the form.
5. Tidy up the names of some of the labels.
6. Change the Artist entry to a drop-down box, to select entries from the *Artist* table.
7. Change the Format entry to a drop-down box, to select entries from the *Format* table.
8. Add a sub-heading above the Tracks subform.
9. Update the fields in the Tracks subform.
10. Change the size of the photo field.
11. Update the *Tab* order of the fields.

To edit the form, right-click on the name and select **Edit** to open the **Database Form** window in edit mode (identifiable by the grid pattern).

8.5.1   Step 1 – Changing the background

To add an image as the background of the form:

1. Right-click on the background and select **Page** from the pop-up menu to open the **Page Style** dialog.
2. Change the **As** dropdown from "Colour" to "Graphic".
3. Click **Browse** to find the graphic file you want to use and click **Open**.
4. Choose whether you want to tile or stretch the image.
5. Click **OK** to close the dialog.

8.5.2   Step 2 – Changing the label colours

You may well find after adding the background image that the colour of the labels means they are now hard to read. To change them:

1. Hold the *Ctrl* key and click on the *AlbumID* label.
2. Right-click and select **Control** to open the **Properties** dialog.

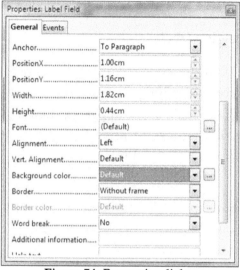

Figure 74: Properties dialog

3. Either click on **Font** or **Background colour** to change the font and label background colours respectively.
4. Close the **Properties** dialog.

Repeat the above for each of the labels.

8.5.3   Step 3 – Rearrange the fields

The fields are currently not well ordered, so we will rearrange them.

1. Click on the *Track* subform to select it and then use the *Down Arrow* key to move it to the bottom of the window.
2. Rearrange the *AlbumTitle*, *Artist*, *Format* and *ReleaseYear* fields so they are in vertical order down the left side of the form.
3. Move the *Photo* field to the top right of the form.

8.5.4 Step 4 – Adding a heading to the form

The easiest way to add and position a heading is to use a textbox from the **Drawing** toolbar.

Draw a textbox where you want to position the heading and then type "Albums". You can then use the **Character** icon on the **Text Object** toolbar to change the size, font and colour of the heading.

8.5.5 Step 5 – Changing labels

Currently, the labels all have the field names, we will change them to something more meaningful.

1. Hold down the *Ctrl* key and click on the *AlbumTitle* label.
2. Right-click and select **Control** to open the **Properties** dialog.
3. Change the label to "Album Title".
4. Close the **Properties** dialog.

Repeat the above to change the *ReleaseYear* label to "Released" and the *Photo* label to "Album Cover".

8.5.6 Step 6 – Changing Artist field to a List Box

Currently, the artist field is just a text entry field, which could take any numeric value. This could lead to albums being entered that are not correctly related to Artists. We will add a List Box that takes its entries from the Album table.

1. Hold down the *Ctrl* key and click on the *Artist* field.
2. Right-click and select **Replace with > List Box**.
3. Right-click and select **Control** to open the **Properties** dialog.
4. On the **General** tab, scroll down and find the **Dropdown** selection and change it from No to Yes.
5. Click on the **Data** tab.
6. Change **Type of list contents** to *Sql*.
7. Type the following in the **List content** field – SELECT ArtistName, ArtistID FROM Artist ORDER BY ArtistName.
8. Ensure that the **Bound field** value is set to 1.
9. Close the **Properties** dialog
10. Enlarge the List Box so that it is a sufficient width to hold the Artist names by dragging the right-hand green handle.

8.5.7   Step 7 – Changing Format field to a List Box

The format field is also currently just a text entry field, which could take any numeric value. We will therefore need to add a List Box that takes its entries from the Format table.

Follow the instructions in Step 5, but use the Sql – SELECT FormatName, FormatId FROM Format ORDER BY FormatName.

8.5.8   Step 8 – Adding a sub-heading to the form

We will now add a sub-heading above the subform.

Draw a textbox where you want to position the sub-heading and then type "Album Tracks". You can then use the **Character** icon on the **Text Object** toolbar to change the size, font and colour of the heading.

8.5.9   Step 9 – Update the fields in the Tracks subform

We will now tidy up the fields in the Tracks subform.

1. Right-click on the *TrackName* field and select **Column** to open the **Properties** dialog and change the **Label** to "Track Name". Then close the dialog.
2. Right-click on the *Length* field and select **Column** to open the **Properties** dialog and change the **Label** to "Track Length". Then close the dialog.
3. Enlarge the fields by clicking on their borders and moving it to the right.

8.5.10   Step 10 – Change the size of the Album Cover field

We will now enlarge the *Album Cover* field.

1. Hold down *CTRL* and click on the *Album Cover* field.
2. Hold one of the green handles and enlarge the field until it is the size you want it.

8.5.11 Step 11 – Change the tab order

We need to change the order that the fields are selected when *Tab* is pressed.

Click on the **Activation Order** icon  to open the **Tab Order** dialog.

Figure 75: Tab Order dialog

Use the **Move Up** and **Move Down** buttons to arrange the controls in the following order:

- txtAlbumTitle
- fmtArtist
- fmtFormat
- fmtReleaseYear
- imgPhoto

Press **OK** to close the dialog.

Close and save the form and then open it in view mode. You should end up with a form that looks similar to the below.

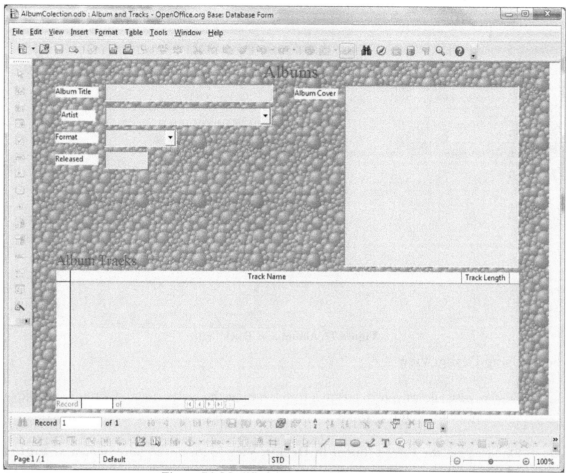

Figure 76: Modified Album and Tracks form

Use your new form to enter a few Albums and their associated Tracks and then view the *Album* and *Track* tables. You should end up with something like the following.

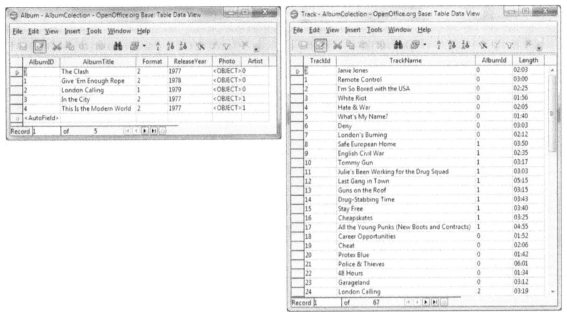

Figure 77: Album and Track tables

8.6 Using Design View

Design view allows you to create a form without the restrictions of wizard and allows you to place the controls wherever you want within the form.

On selecting the **Create Form in Design View** option, the same screen as **Figure 73** will be shown, but with no content. You can then use the tools on the menu on the left to add controls to the form.

When you have added your first control, right-click on it and select the **Form** option from the context menu to open the **Form Properties** dialog

Figure 78: Form Properties dialog

We need to select the table that will be used as the basis of the form:

1. Change the **Content type** dropdown to *Table*.
2. Select the table to use in the **Content** dropdown.
3. Close the dialog.

We can now select the field that will be used with the control. Right/click on the control again and select **Control** from the context menu to open the **Properties** dialog.

Figure 79: Properties dialog

Change the **Data field** dropdown to the field that you want this control to populate.

James Steinberg

9   QUERIES

9.1   Introduction

As mentioned earlier in this chapter, queries allow you to get information from a database in a specific way, by creating a temporary table containing the required data.

Base provides three methods to query the data:

- The Query Wizard
- The Query Design view.
- SQL View

The first two options provide a graphical means of producing a query, but the underlying query will be defined in SQL

9.2   Using the Query Wizard

We will use the query wizard to display all of the *Tracks* ordered by *Length*.

9.2.1   Step 1 – Selecting the fields

On the main Base page. Click on the Queries icon and then select **Use Wizard to Create Query**, to open the first page of the **Query Wizard**.

Figure 80: Query Wizard page 1

We want the name of a *Track* and its *Length*, so first select the *Track* table in the
Tables section and move the *TrackName* and *Length* fields to the **Fields in the
Query** section using the **>** button. Then press **Next**

9.2.2   Step 2 – Sorting the data

You should now be on page 2 of the Query Wizard.

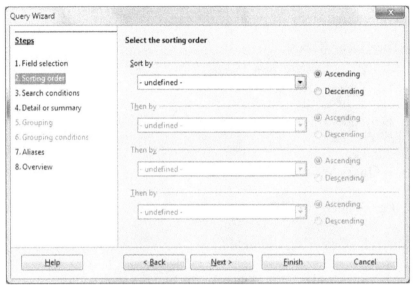

Figure 81: Query Wizard page 2

We will sort our results by increasing *Length*, so in the **Sort by** dropdown select
Track.Length and press **Next**.

9.2.3 Step 3 – Searching the data

You should now be on page 3 of the Query Wizard.

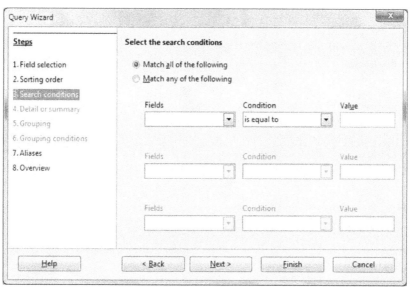

Figure 82: Query Wizard page 3

Base allows us to filter the returned data on a number of criteria using different criteria. For the purpose of this example, we want to return all the tracks, so just press **Next**.

9.2.4   Step 4 – Detail or Summary

You should now be on page 4 of the Query Wizard.

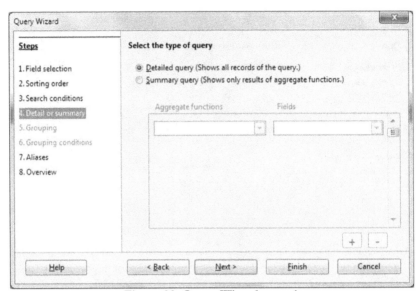

Figure 83: Query Wizard page 4

This page allows you to specify whether you want to use functions to Aggregate the data (i.e. provide a sum of a particular field). For the purpose of this example, we want to return a detailed query, so just press **Next**.

9.2.5 Step 5 – Aliases

You should now be on page 7 of the Query Wizard.

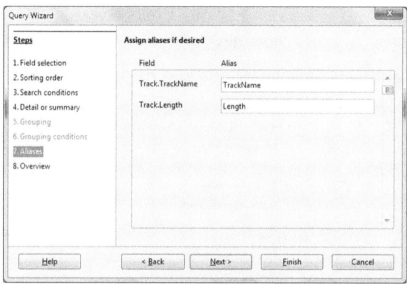

Figure 84: Query Wizard page 7

This page allows you to rename fields for the purpose of presentation. Add a space to the *TrackName* field to tidy it up and then press **Next**.

9.2.6 Step 6 – Overview

You should now be on page 8 of the Query Wizard.

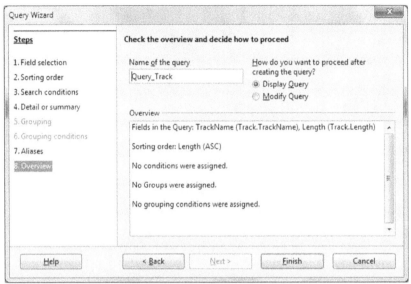

Figure 85: Query Wizard page 8

This page provides an overview of the query you have created and allows you to give it a name. Change the name to "Tracks by Length" and press **Finish**.

The **Table Data View** window will open displaying something like the following.

Figure 86: Results of "Tracks by Length" query

9.3 Using the Query Design View

We will use the **Query Design View** to create a query that will list the number of tracks released by a particular artist.

Click on **Create Query in Design View** to open the **Query Design** window and **Add Table or Query** dialog.

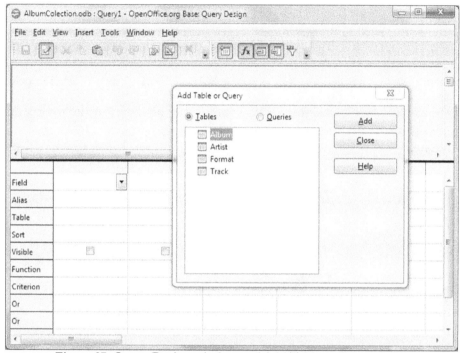

Figure 87: Query Design window and Add Table or Query dialog

For our query, we will obviously need the *Artist* and *Track* tables, but we will also need the *Album* table as that provides a link between artist and track. So select all three tables either by double clicking on them or clicking and pressing **Add** then close the dialog.

The top section of the **Query Design** window shows the selected tables and the relationships between them. The bottom half is where we design our query.

Start of by selecting *Artist.ArtistName* in the first **Field** drop-down and then enter "Artist Name" in the **Alias** field. In the **Sort** field select "ascending" and in the **Function** field select "Group".

Now move to the second column and select *Track.TrackName* and enter "No. of Tracks" in the **Alias** field. Then in the **Function** field select "Count"

Your query design should now look like this.

Field	ArtistName	TrackName
Alias	Artist Name	No. of Tracks
Table		
Sort	ascending	
Visible	☑	☑
Function	Group	Count
Criterion		
Or		

Figure 88: Query Design for No. of Tracks query

You can now run your query by selecting **Edit > Run Query** or clicking on the **Run Query** icon 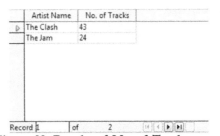. This will display the results of your query at the top of the window in a new section.

Artist Name	No. of Tracks
The Clash	43
The Jam	24

Record 1   of   2

Figure 89: Results of No. of Tracks query

Save the query as "No. of Tracks" and then close the window.

9.4   Using the SQL View

SQL is the language that is used to generate all the queries within Base. The queries that we have so far created using the **Query Wizard** and **Query Design** are converted into SQL to produce the results. SQL can be used to create complex queries.

You can see the underlying SQL by right clicking on a query and selecting **Edit in SQL View**. This is what the Tracks by Length query looks like.

```
SELECT "TrackName" AS "Track Name", "Length" AS "Length" FROM "Track" ORDER
BY "Length" ASC
```

The words in UPPERCASE are SQL keywords and the words in quotes refer to tables, fields or conditions.

We will not go into depth on the syntax of SQL here, the next chapter will cover the basics and there are many books and websites on the subject if you want to know more.

We will use the SQL View to design a query that lists the Artists, Albums and the number of Tracks on the Album for each Album that is owned on Vinyl

Click on **Create Query in SQL View** and the **Query Design** window will open with just a blank text entry area. This is where you will type your query.

Type the word SELECT followed by a space and you will see that it changes colour to blue to indicate that it has been identified as a keyword.

Now type "ArtistName", "AlbumTitle", COUNT("TrackName") AS "No. of Tracks" followed by *Return*. COUNT and AS are keywords, so they have turned blue. COUNT will return a number of records that meet a given criteria and AS allows us to rename a field. The field and table names have to be surrounded by double quotes.

Now type FROM "Artist", "Album", "Track", "Format" followed by *Return*. Again, FROM is a keyword and specifies which tables we are going to be working with.

We will now define a number of conditions, including how the table join together and how to limit the rows returned. Type WHERE "Album"."Artist" = "Artist"."ArtistID" and press *Return*. WHERE is always used to introduce the first condition. In this case we are linking the *Album* and *Artist* tables using the Id field.

We will now link the other tables together, so type the following on separate lines AND "Track"."AlbumId" = "Album"."AlbumID" and AND "Format"."FormatId" = "Album"."Format".

The final condition is the one to limit the results to just vinyl albums, so add the following as a new line AND "Format"."FormatName" = 'Vinyl'. Vinyl is a text string, so it is enclosed in single quotes.

Finally, we will define how the records should be grouped together for the purpose of the count. Type the following on a new line GROUP BY "ArtistName", "AlbumTitle".

Your query should now look like this:

```
SELECT "ArtistName", "AlbumTitle", COUNT("TrackName") AS "No. of Tracks"
FROM "Artist", "Album", "Track", "Format"
WHERE "Album"."Artist" = "Artist"."ArtistID"
AND "Track"."AlbumId" = "Album"."AlbumID"
AND "Format"."FormatId" = "Album"."Format"
AND "Format"."FormatName" = 'Vinyl'
GROUP BY "ArtistName", "AlbumTitle"
```

You can now run your query by selecting **Edit > Run Query** or clicking on the **Run Query** icon. This will display the results of your query at the top of the window in a new section.

ArtistName	AlbumTitle	No. of Tracks
The Clash	The Clash	14
The Clash	Give 'Em Enough Rope	10
The Jam	In the City	12
The Jam	This Is the Modern World	12

Record 1   of   4

Figure 90: Results of No. of Tracks by Album query

Save the query as "No. of Tracks by Album" and then close the window.

10 INTRODUCION TO SQL

10.1 Introduction

SQL stands for Structured Query Language and is a language specifically designed for accessing and manipulating databases. There are commands for creating and updating tables, as well as retrieving the information from them.

This chapter acts as an introduction to the subject and as such will only cover the creation of commands for retrieving data from them. If you want to know more about creating and updating tables then there are many general SQL books available.

10.2 SELECT FROM statement

The most basic form of an SQL query is **SELECT [columns] FROM [table]**, which will display the data in the requested columns for every row in the specified table. For example, the query:

```
SELECT AlbumName, Released
FROM Album;
```

Would result in the something similar to the following being returned.

AlbumName	Released
The Clash	1977
Give 'Em Enough Rope	1978
London Calling	1979
In the City	1977
This is the Modern World	1977

If you want to return all of the columns in a table, you can use * in place of the list of columns, for example:

```
SELECT *
FROM Album;
```

10.2.1 SELECT DISTINCT

If you have a table that has a number of duplicate entries in it and you only want to return the distinct values, you can add the DISTINCT keyword to your query so that it looks like this: **SELECT DISTINCT [columns] FROM [table]**.

10.3 WHERE and AND & OR clauses

The WHERE, AND and OR clauses are used to filter records that match a particular criteria. The first criteria is specified using the WHERE clause and subsequent ones using AND or OR clauses.

These clauses can also be used for joining tables (more on this in section 10.6).

10.3.1 WHERE clause

The format of the WHERE clause is WHERE [column_name] [operator] [value]. For example:

```
SELECT AlbumName, Released
FROM Album
WHERE Released = 1977;
```

Would result in something similar to the following being returned.

AlbumName	Released
The Clash	1977
In the City	1977
This is the Modern World	1977

10.3.2 AND & OR clauses

AND and OR conditions work in the same way as the WHERE clause, but are used to add additional conditions. Their formats are AND [column_name] [operator[[value] and OR [column_name] [operator[[value].

An example of using the AND clause is

```
SELECT AlbumName, Released
FROM Album
WHERE Released = 1977
AND Artist = 1;
```

Which will return something like the following:

AlbumName	Released
In the City	1977
This is the Modern World	1977

An example of using the OR clause is

```
SELECT AlbumName, Released
FROM Album
WHERE Released = 1977
OR Released = 1978;
```

Which will return something like the following:

AlbumName	Released
The Clash	1977
Give 'Em Enough Rope	1978
In the City	1977
This is the Modern World	1977

10.3.3 Operators

SQL supports a number of operators that can be used in the WHERE, AND and OR clauses:

Operator	Description
=	Equal to
<> or !=	Not equal to
>	Greater than
<	Less than
>=	Greater than or equal
<=	Less than or equal
BETWEEN	Between an inclusive range
LIKE	Matching a pattern
IN	Matches one of a list of possible values

10.4 ORDER BY clause

The ORDER BY clause is used to sort the returned records into a particular order. The format of the ORDER BY clause is ORDER BY [columns] ASC|DESC. For example:

```
SELECT AlbumName, Released
FROM Album
ORDER BY Released, AlbumName ASC
```

Which will return something like the following:

AlbumName	Released
In the City	1977
The Clash	1977
This is the Modern World	1977
Give 'Em Enough Rope	1978
London Calling	1979

10.5 Aggregation

Up to now, all the queries we have written have just returned a selection of records from the table that was being queried. SQL also supports a number of aggregate functions that will return things like sums and counts of records. The aggregate functions that are provided are shown in the table below.

Function	Description
AVG()	Returns the average value.
COUNT()	Returns a count of the number of records.
FIRST()	Returns the first record.
LAST()	Returns the last record.
MAX()	Returns the largest record.
MIN()	Returns the smallest record.
SUM()	Returns the sum of the values.

The aggregate function is put in the column list and a column name put in the brackets. For example:

```
SELECT COUNT(*)
FROM Album
WHERE Released = 1977;
```

Which would return something like the following:

COUNT(*)
3

10.5.1 GROUPing records

When using aggregation functions, it can also be useful to group your records so that for example you can get a count of records in a particular category. This can be done using the **GROUP BY** clause, which has the following format **GROUP BY [columns]**. For example:

```
SELECT Released, COUNT(*)
FROM Album
GROUP BY Released;
```

Would return something like the following:

Released	COUNT(*)
1977	3
1978	1
1979	1

10.5.2 HAVING clause

The **WHERE** clause does not work with the aggregate functions, so if you want to add a condition to an aggregate, you will need to use the **HAVING** clause. The **HAVING** clause has the following format **HAVING aggregate_function(column) operator value**. For example:

```
SELECT Released, COUNT(*)
FROM Album
GROUP BY Released
HAVING COUNT(*) > 1;
```

Which would return the following:

Released	COUNT(*)
1977	3

10.6 Joining tables

So far, all the queries that we have written in this chapter have only involved using one table. The power of SQL is that it can combine multiple tables to provide a composite result. This is achieved by joining the tables.

SQL supports four different types of joins:

- INNER JOIN: Returns all rows when there is at least one match in BOTH tables
- LEFT JOIN: Return all rows from the left table, and the matched rows from the right table
- RIGHT JOIN: Return all rows from the right table, and the matched rows from the left table
- FULL JOIN: Return all rows when there is a match in ONE of the tables

10.6.1 INNER JOIN

The INNER JOIN keyword selects all rows from both tables as long as there is a match between the columns in both tables.

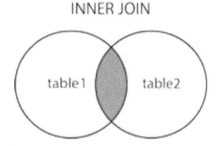

There are two ways of specifying an inner join. The first is using a WHERE (or AND) clause: WHERE table1.column_name = table2.column_name and the second is using the INNER JOIN (or just JOIN) keyword: FROM table1 INNER JOIN table2 ON table1.column_name = table2.column_name. The following example shows both methods:

```
SELECT AlbumName, ArtistName
FROM Album, Artist
WHERE Album.ArtistId = Artist.ArtistId;

SELECT AlbumName, ArtistName
FROM Album
INNER JOIN Artist
ON Album.ArtistId = Artist.ArtistId;
```

The results of both queries would be:

AlbumName	ArtistName
The Clash	The Clash
Give 'Em Enough Rope	The Clash
London Calling	The Clash
In The City	The Jam
This is the Modern World	The Jam

10.6.2 LEFT JOIN

The **LEFT JOIN** keyword returns all rows from the left table (table1), with the matching rows in the right table (table2). The result is NULL in the right side when there is no match.

LEFT JOIN

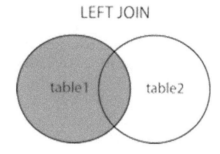

The format of a **LEFT JOIN** is FROM table1 LEFT JOIN table2 ON table1.column_name = table2.column_name. In some database systems, LEFT JOIN is referred to as **LEFT OUTER JOIN**. For example:

```
SELECT ArtistName, AlbumName
FROM Artist
LEFT JOIN Album
ON Artist.ArtistId = Album.ArtistId;
```

The results of the above would be:

ArtistName	AlbumName
The Clash	The Clash
The Clash	Give 'Em Enough Rope
The Clash	London Calling
The Jam	In The City
The Jam	This is the Modern World
Kraftwerk	

10.6.3 RIGHT JOIN

The RIGHT JOIN keyword returns all rows from the right table (table2), with the matching rows in the left table (table1). The result is NULL in the left side when there is no match.

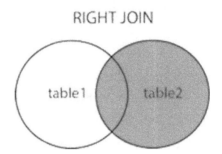

RIGHT JOIN

The format of a RIGHT JOIN is FROM table1 RIGHT JOIN table2 ON table1.column_name = table2.column_name. In some database systems, RIGHT JOIN is referred to as RIGHT OUTER JOIN. For example:

```
SELECT AlbumName, ArtistName
FROM Album
RIGHT JOIN Artist
ON Artist.ArtistId = Album.ArtistId;
```

The results of the above would be:

ArtistName	AlbumName
The Clash	The Clash
The Clash	Give 'Em Enough Rope
The Clash	London Calling
The Jam	In The City
The Jam	This is the Modern World
Kraftwerk	

10.6.4 FULL OUTER JOIN

The FULL OUTER JOIN keyword returns all rows from the left table (table1) and from the right table (table2). The FULL OUTER JOIN keyword combines the result of both LEFT and RIGHT joins.

FULL OUTER JOIN

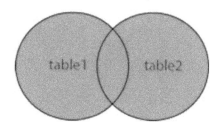

The format of a FULL OUTER JOIN is FROM table1 FULL OUTER JOIN table2 ON table1.column_name = table2.column_name. For example:

```
SELECT ArtistName, AlbumName
FROM Artist
FULL OUTER JOIN Album
ON Artist.ArtistId = Album.ArtistId;
```

The results of the above would be:

ArtistName	AlbumName
The Clash	The Clash
The Clash	Give 'Em Enough Rope
The Clash	London Calling
The Jam	In The City
The Jam	This is the Modern World
Kraftwerk	
	Unknown Pleasures

James Steinberg

11 REPORTS

11.1 Generating reports

Reports are a means of presenting the information in the database in a useful way, which is printable. Reports are either generated from the contents of a single table or a query. Reports can either be Static or Dynamic. A static report is based on data at the time the report was created, whereas a dynamic report can be updated to show the current data.

Reports are created using the **Report Wizard**, which we will use to produce a report showing the results of our No. of Tracks by Album query that we created in section 9.4.

11.2 Using the Report Wizard

11.2.1 Step 1 – Field Selection

Click on the **Reports** icon on the Base main page and select **Use Wizard to Create Report** to open the **Report Wizard**.

Figure 91: Report Wizard page 1

Select the No of Tracks by Album query in the **Tables or queries** section to display the fields available and click on the **>>** button to select all of the fields. Then press **Next**.

11.2.2 Step 2 – Field Selection

You should now be on page 2 of the wizard.

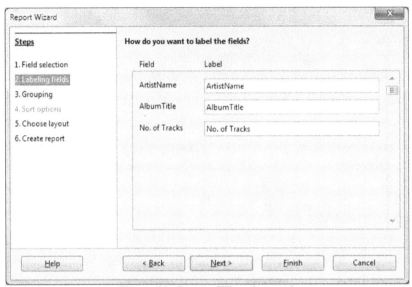

Figure 92: Report Wizard page 2

Tidy up the Labels by putting spaces in them and then press **Next**.

11.2.3   Step 3 – Grouping

You should now be on page 3 of the wizard.

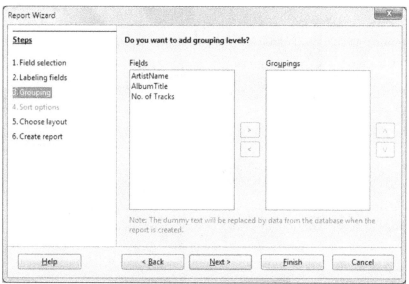

Figure 93: Report Wizard page 3

This page allows you to group the data if required. We have already taken care of this in our query, so just press **Next**.

11.2.4 Step 4 – Choose layout

You should now be on page 5 of the wizard.

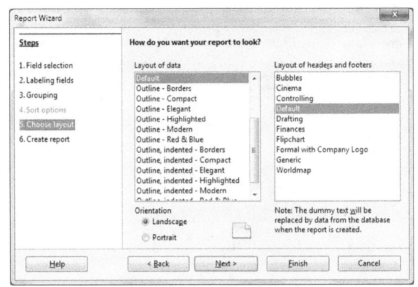

Figure 94: Report Wizard page 5

Choose a suitable layout (your choice will update on the specimen report in the background) and press **Next**.

11.2.5 Step 5 – Create report

You should now be on page 6 of the wizard.

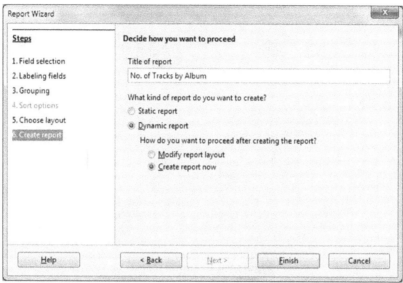

Figure 95: Report Wizard page 6

Here you can name your report and also choose whether it should be Static or Dynamic.

Click on the **Finish** button to create the report, which will look like this:

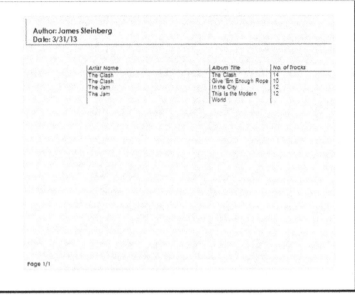

Author: James Steinberg
Date: 3/31/13

Artist Name	Album Title	No. of Tracks
The Clash	The Clash	14
The Clash	Give 'Em Enough Rope	10
The Jam	In the City	12
The Jam	This Is the Modern World	12

Page 1/1

Figure 96: Example report

11.3 Editing reports

Once you have created your report using the **Report Wizard**, you can tidy it up by right clicking on its name and selecting **Edit** to open the **Report Design** window.

For example, if you look at our report above, you will see that the data format could do with correction, as could the width of the columns.

To reformat the date field into a more readable format right-click on it and select **Fields** to open the **Edit Fields** dialog

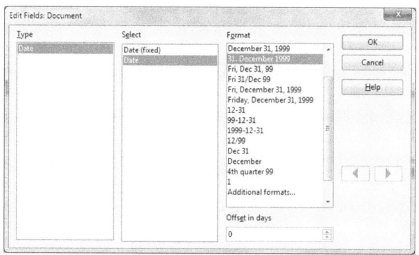
Figure 97: Edit Fields dialog

Change the format in the **Format** field to something more suitable and then click OK to close the dialog.

To change the width of the columns, put the mouse pointer over one of the column borders and the pointer will change. You can then drag the column to the required width.

James Steinberg

12 OTHER DATA SOURCES

12.1 Registering other data sources

Base will allow you to open a database that is not in the OpenOffice.org *.odb format.

This is done using the **Database Wizard** and using the **Connect to an existing database** option. Choose the type of database by clicking on the down arrow next to **Database Type** and then click **Next**. You will then have to provide the connection details dependant on the type of database (such as username and password). Once you have connected then you can register the database so that it is available in other OpenOffice.org programs.

12.1.1 Connecting to a spreadsheet as a data source

For example, to connect to a Calc spreadsheet as a data source, do the following.

1. Select **File > New > Database**.
2. Select **Connect to an existing database** and select *Spreadsheet* as the **Database Type**. Then click **Next**.
3. Use **Browse** to find the database you want to access. Then click **Next**.
4. You can then choose whether to register the new database and click **Finish** to save the database and open it for editing.

All of the sheets in the spreadsheet will be imported as a separate table.

12.1.2 Registering *.odb databases

*.odb files (OpenDocument Base format) can be created by other applications and it is possible to register these from within Base.

1. Select **Tools > Options > OpenOffice.org Base > Databases**.
2. Click on **New**.
3. Use **Browse** to locate the database file.
4. Enter the registered name and press **OK**.

13. CUSTOMISING BASE

13.1 Introduction

OpenOffice.org provides the facilities to make a number of customisations to its components. In Base, you can customise menus, toolbars and keyboard shortcuts and assign macros to events.

This chapter describes the customisations that can be made using the **Customise** dialog.

13.2 Customising the menu bar

You can add and rearrange the menus and add commands to the menus. Changes to the menus are made using the **Menus** tab of the **Customise** dialog, which can be opened using the **Tools > Customise** option.

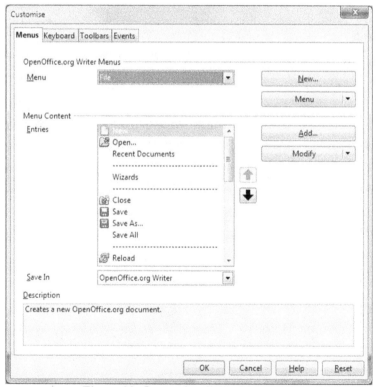

Figure 98: Customise dialog Menus tab

13.2.1 Adding a new menu

To add a new menu, click on the **New** button to open the **New Menu** dialog.

Figure 99: New Menu dialog

Type the name of your new menu in the **Menu name** box and it will appear in the **Menu position** list. You can then use the up and down arrow buttons to move it to the correct position on the menu bar. When you have finished click **OK** to close the dialog.

Your new menu will now appear in the **Customise** dialog, but will not appear on the menu bar until you click **OK** on the **Customise** dialog.

You can now add commands to the new menu, as described in section 0.

13.2.2 Adding a command to a menu

To add a new command to a menu:

1. Select the menu in the **Menu** drop down.
2. Click the **Add** button to open the **Add Commands** dialog.

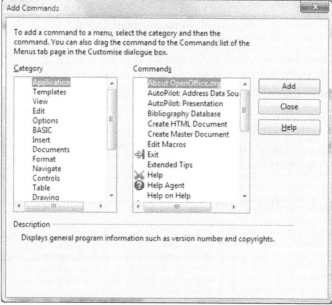

Figure 100: Add Commands dialog

3. Select the category of command to add from the **Category** list.
4. Select the command from the **Commands** list.
5. Click the **Add** button to add the command.
6. Repeat steps 3 to 5 to add any other commands.
7. Click **Close** to close the dialog when you are finished.

Back on the **Customise** dialog, you can use the up and down arrow buttons next to the **Entries** list to arrange the commands in the required sequence.

13.2.3 Modifying existing menus

To modify an existing menu, select it in the **Menu** drop down and then click the **Menu** button to display a list of modifications – **Move**, **Rename** and **Delete**.

To move a menu, select **Menu > Move** and the **Move Menu** dialog will be opened, which is similar to that shown in Figure 99, but without the **Menu name** box. You can use the up and down arrow buttons to rearrange the order of the menu items. To move a submenu, select the main menu in the **Menu** dropdown and then select the submenu in the **Entries** list. You can then use the arrow buttons next to the **Entries** list to move the submenu.

To rename a menu, select **Menu > Rename** to open the **Rename Menu** dialog.

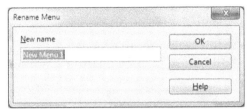

Figure 101: Rename Menu dialog

You can also use this option to specify a keyboard shortcut for an entry, by adding a tilde (~) in front of the letter you want to use as a shortcut. It is not possible to rename the standard OpenOffice.org menus.

To delete a menu, select **Menu > Delete** to delete the selected menu. Be careful with this option as it does not ask for confirmation before deleting. It is not possible to delete the standard OpenOffice.org menus.

13.2.4 Modifying menu entries

You can modify menu entries by selecting the entry and then clicking the **Modify** button to display a list of modifications – **Add Sub-menu, Begin a Group, Rename** and **Delete**.

The **Add Sub-menu** option will open the **Add Sub-menu** dialog, where you can name your sub-menu.

Figure 102: Add Sub-menu dialog

The **Begin a Group** option will insert a divider below the currently selected entry.

The **Rename** option will open the **Rename Menu** dialog (Figure 101) to enable you to rename the menu entry.

The **Delete** option will delete the menu entry – again without a confirmation dialog being displayed.

13.3 Assigning shortcut keys

You can define your own shortcuts and assign them to the standard OpenOffice.org functions or to your own macros. These can also be saved for use with the entire OpenOffice.org suite.

Changes to the keyboard assignments are made using the **Keyboard** tab of the **Customise** dialog, which can be opened using the **Tools > Customise** option.

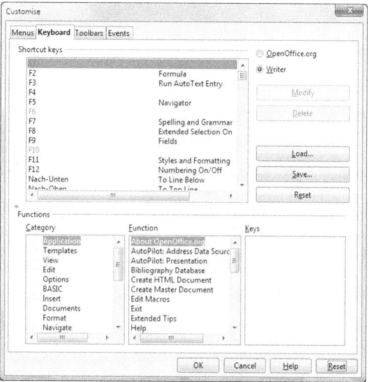

Figure 103: Customise dialog Keyboard tab

13.3.1 Assigning OpenOffice.org commands to a shortcut key

To assign a standard OpenOffice.org function to a key:

1. Select whether to assign the shortcut key in all components of OpenOffice.org or just in Writer, by using the **OpenOffice.org** or **Writer** options.
2. Select the desired shortcut key in the **Shortcut keys** list.
3. Use the **Category** and **Function** lists to find the command that you want assign.
4. Press the **Modify** button to assign the command and it will appear in the **Keys** list in the bottom right of the dialog.
5. Press the **OK** button to accept the change and close the dialog.

13.3.2 Assigning macros to a shortcut key

You can record or manually write your own macros to perform repetitive and often used tasks quickly. These macros can then be assigned to a keyboard shortcut.

To assign the macro to a shortcut key, follow the instructions in section 13.3.1 and locate the macro in the "OpenOffice.org Macros" category on the **Category** and **Function** lists.

13.3.3 Assigning styles to a shortcut key

Styles can also be assigned to shortcut keys to allow them to be quickly assigned. There are a number of pre-defined shortcuts, such as *Ctrl+0* for the *Text body* and *Ctrl+1* for the *Heading 1* paragraph styles. You can modify these shortcuts as well as defining your own.

To assign a style to a shortcut key, follow the instructions in section 13.3.1 and locate the style under the Styles category in the **Category** and **Function** lists.

13.3.4 Saving keyboard configurations to a files

You can save your keyboard shortcuts to a file to allow you to reload them at a later date. To do this, use the **Save** button to open the (incorrectly named ☺) **Load Keyboard Configuration** dialog. You can then save the file in the normal way, either as a new file or overwriting an existing file.

13.3.5 Loading a saved keyboard configuration

You can load your previously saved keyboard shortcuts using the **Load** button to open the **Load Keyboard Configuration** dialog. You can then load the file in the normal way.

13.3.6 Resetting shortcut keys

You can use the **Reset** button to reseat all of the keyboard shortcuts to their default values. Care should be taken with this feature as no confirmation dialog box is displayed before the reset is performed.

13.4 Customising toolbars

You can create new tool bars and also add and delete icons from the list of those available for a particular toolbar. Changes to the toolbars are made using the **Toolbars** tab of the **Customise** dialog, which can be opened using the **Tools > Customise** option.

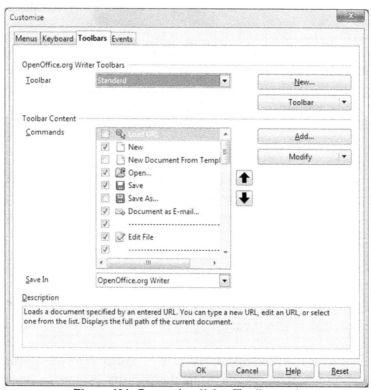

Figure 104: Customise dialog Toolbars tab

13.4.1 Adding a new toolbar

To add a new menu, click on the **New** button to open the **Name** dialog.

Figure 105: Name dialog

You can then name your toolbar and decide where to save it. Then click **OK** to close the dialog. Your new toolbar will now appear in the **Customise** dialog.

You can now add commands to the new toolbar, as described in section 13.4.2.

13.4.2 Adding a command to a toolbar

The commands that are shown for a particular toolbar are only a subset of those that are actually available. You can click the down arrow at the right-hand end of the toolbar to show the full list of available commands and select them for display in the toolbar.

You can also add additional commands to the list of available commands for a toolbar, by clicking the **Add** button in the **Toolbar Content** section of the dialog. This will open the **Add Commands** dialog, which is the same as that for adding a command to a menu (Figure 100). Once you have added all your commands, click **Close** to go back to the **Customise** dialog and then use the up and down arrow buttons to arrange the commands in the right sequence. You can then click **OK** to close the **Customise** dialog.

When you add the commands, you will see that some of them have icons beside them and some do not. If you choose a command without an icon then the toolbar will display the full name of the command. You can add your own icon to the command as described in section 13.4.3.

13.4.3 Choosing icons for toolbar commands

Toolbars normally show an icon rather than words, but not all of the commands have an icon associated with them.

To add an icon to a command, select the command in the **Commands** list and then use the **Change icon** option from the **Modify** button to open the **Change Icon** dialog.

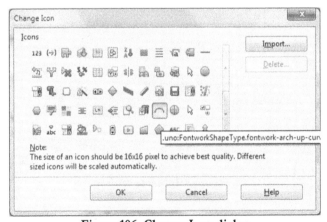

Figure 106: Change Icon dialog

You can select one of the pre-defined icons, by clicking on it and then clicking the **OK** button.

If you have a custom icon that you have created, then you can import it using the **Import** button and navigating to its location. Custom icons should be either 16x16 or 26x26 pixels in size and have a maximum of 256 colours. You can delete a custom icon by selecting it and pressing the **Delete** button.

13.4.4 Modifying an existing toolbar

The **Toolbar** button provides a number of commands for modifying the toolbar.

The **Rename** option opens the **Rename Toolbar** dialog, which looks the same as the **Rename Menu** dialog. This option is not available for standard OpenOffice.org toolbars.

The **Delete** option will delete the currently selected toolbar. This option does not ask for confirmation before deleting the toolbar. It is not possible to delete the standard OpenOffice.org toolbars.

The **Restore Default Settings** will restore the default settings for the selected toolbar.

The remaining three options – **Icons only**, **Text only** and **Icons & Text** determine what is shown on the toolbar.

13.4.5 Modifying commands

The **Modify** button provides a number of commands for modifying the individual selected command.

The **Rename** option will open the **Rename Toolbar** dialog (which looks similar to Figure 101) to enable you to rename the command.

The **Delete** option will delete the command – again without a confirmation dialog being displayed.

The **Restore Default Command** option will restore the default settings for the selected command.

The **Begin a Group** option will insert a divider below the currently selected entry.

The **Change Icon** option allows you to change the icon for the command, as described in section 13.4.3, while the **Reset Icon** option will reset the icon to the default icon.

13.5 Assigning macros to events

OpenOffice.org can use events to drive the execution of a macro. An event is something that happens, such as a document being opened or a key being pressed. Each event can be assigned a different macro that will run each time the event occurs.

Changes to the keyboard assignments are made using the **Events** tab of the **Customise** dialog, which can be opened using the **Tools > Customise** option.

Figure 107: Customise dialog Events tab

To assign a macro to an event, highlight the event and then click the **Macro** button and use the **Macro Selector** dialog to navigate to the required macro. When you have assigned all the macros you want to, click the **OK** button to close the dialog.

13.6 Using extensions to add functionality

Extensions are packages that can be installed in OpenOffice.org to add new functionality. Extensions are available from a number or places, but the official OpenOffice.org extension repository can be found at http://extensions.services.openoffice.org/. Some extensions are provided free of charge, while others are available for a fee.

13.6.1 Installing extensions

To install an extension, you will first need to download it from the Internet and then you can install it as follows:

1. Select **Tools > Extension Manager** to open the **Extension Manager** window.

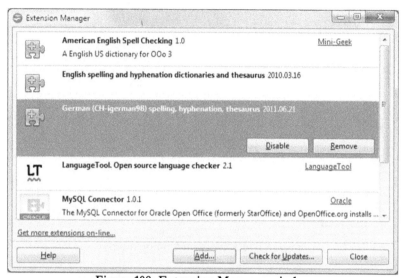

Figure 108: Extension Manager window

2. Click on the **Add** button and a file browser window will open. Find and select the extension and click **Open** and the extension will be installed.

13.6.2 Removing and disabling extensions

You can remove or disable extensions from the **Extension Manager** dialog by selecting the extension and then clicking the **Remove** or **Disable** buttons.

13.6.3 Updating extensions

If you are connected to the Internet, you can check for updates in your installed extensions by pressing the **Check for Updates** button. This will open the **Extension Update** dialog.

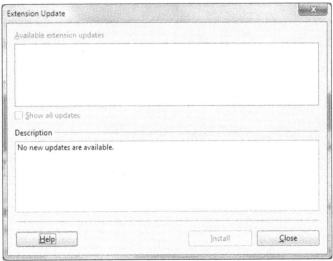

Figure 109: Extension Update dialog

If any updates are available you can use the **Install** button to install them.

INDEX

ABOUT THE AUTHOR

Professor James Steinberg is a Professor of Applied Computing, lecturing on programming in a number of current and historical programming languages.

Professor Steinberg also acts in a consultancy role for a number of software development companies, advising on the implementation of corporate systems.

Professor Steinberg is an avid proponent of the Open Source movement and regularly lectures on the benefits of the Open Source paradigm.

Professor Steinberg is married with two children.

More information about Professor Steinberg and the other books he has written can be found at http://www.jamessteinberg.info.

OTHER BOOKS BY THE AUTHOR

Open Office Basic: An Introduction

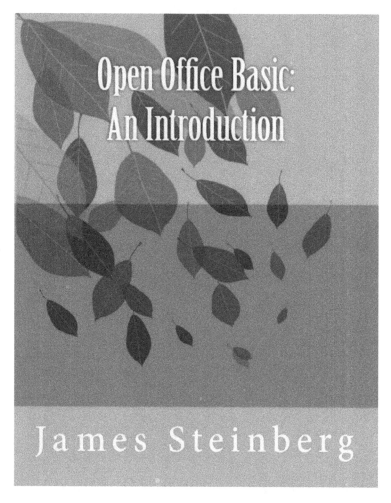

Apache Open Office is the leading open-source office software suite. It features word processing, spreadsheets, presentations, graphics and databases. It is available for all major operating systems. Open Office has the ability to automate features using recorded and manually created macros, created using a number of different programming languages. This book concentrates on one of those languages OpenOffice.org Basic. This book starts by giving an overview of the language and its structure, before detailing the various commands and functions that are available in OpenOffice.org Basic.

Open Office Basic: An Introduction is available in Paperback (ISBN 1481270931) and as a Kindle eBook from your local Amazon website.

OTHER BOOKS BY THE AUTHOR

"Hello, World!"
A History of Programming

"Hello, World!" looks at the history of programming from the conceptual days of the 19th Century, through the invention of modern computing to the dawn of the 21st Century.

As well as a detailed journey through the programming languages developed during the 20th and 21st centuries, this book provides a valuable comparison of the syntax of a number of the influential programming languages, using the famous "Hello, World!" code.

"Hello, World!" is available in Paperback (ISBN 1481277154) and as a Kindle eBook from your local Amazon website.

OTHER BOOKS BY THE AUTHOR

OpenOffice.org 3.4: An Introduction

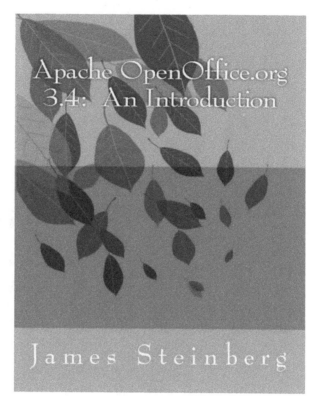

OpenOffice.org is a leading open-source office software suite. It features word processing, spreadsheets, presentations, graphics and databases. It is available for all major operating systems.

This book provides a general introduction to the OpenOffice.org 3.4 suite and the various components that it contains. The book also covers general topics such as setting up and customising OpenOffice.org, working with styles, templates and introducing macros.

OpenOffice.org 3.4: An Introduction is the first book in Professor Steinberg's *Using Apache OpenOffice.org 3.4* series.

OpenOffice.org 3.4: An Introduction is available in Paperback (ISBN 1482534312) and as a Kindle eBook from your local Amazon website.

OTHER BOOKS BY THE AUTHOR

OpenOffice.org 3.4: Using Math

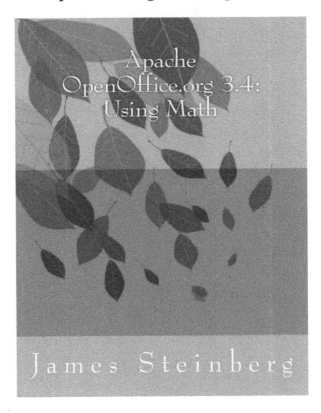

OpenOffice.org is a leading open-source office software suite. It features word processing, spreadsheets, presentations, graphics and databases. It is available for all major operating systems.

This book provides a how-to approach to using Math, which is Apache OpenOffice.org's formula editor. The book details how to build equations and formulas using Math, as well as showing example formulas.

OpenOffice.org 3.4: Using Math is the second book in Professor Steinberg's *Using Apache OpenOffice.org 3.4* series.

OpenOffice.org 3.4: Using Math is available in Paperback (ISBN 1484188713) and as a Kindle eBook from your local Amazon website.

OTHER BOOKS BY THE AUTHOR

OpenOffice.org 3.4: Using Writer

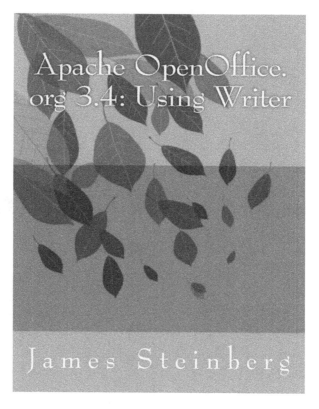

OpenOffice.org is a leading open-source office software suite. It features word processing, spreadsheets, presentations, graphics and databases. It is available for all major operating systems.

This book provides a how-to approach to using Writer, which is Apache OpenOffice.org's word processor.

OpenOffice.org 3.4: Using Writer is the third book in Professor Steinberg's *Using Apache OpenOffice.org 3.4* series.

OpenOffice.org 3.4: Using Writer is available in Paperback (ISBN 1484845293) and as a Kindle eBook from your local Amazon website.

OTHER BOOKS BY THE AUTHOR

OpenOffice.org 3.4: Using Calc

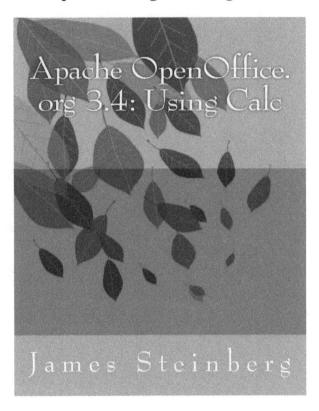

OpenOffice.org is a leading open-source office software suite. It features word processing, spreadsheets, presentations, graphics and databases. It is available for all major operating systems.

This book provides a how-to approach to using Calc, which is Apache OpenOffice.org's spreadsheet application. The book details how to create spreadsheets and charts and use the analysis tools such as Pivot Tables

OpenOffice.org 3.4: Using Writer is the fourth book in Professor Steinberg's *Using Apache OpenOffice.org 3.4* series.

OpenOffice.org 3.4: Using Writer is available in Paperback (ISBN 1490925678) and as a Kindle eBook from your local Amazon website.

OTHER BOOKS BY THE AUTHOR

OpenOffice.org 3.4: Little Book of Calc Functions

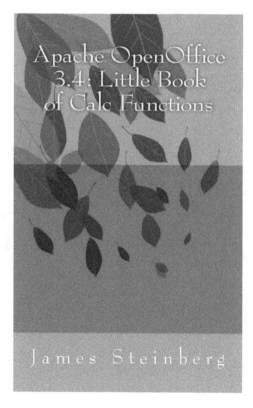

OpenOffice.org is a leading open-source office software suite. It features word processing, spreadsheets, presentations, graphics and databases. It is available for all major operating systems.

This book provides details of the functions provided by Calc, which is OpenOffice.org's spreadsheet application. The functions are split as per the categories in the Function Wizard and then organised in alphabetical order per category. A full alphabetical index is also provided for ease of look up.

OpenOffice.org 3.4: Little Book of Calc Functions is the fifth book in Professor Steinberg's *Using Apache OpenOffice.org 3.4* series.

OpenOffice.org 3.4: Little Book of Calc Functions is available in Paperback (ISBN 1491235608) and as a Kindle eBook from your local Amazon website.

OTHER BOOKS BY THE AUTHOR

OpenOffice.org 3.4: Using Impress

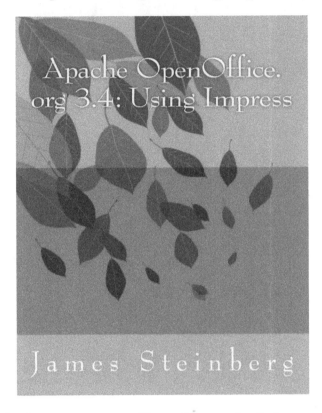

OpenOffice.org is a leading open-source office software suite. It features word processing, spreadsheets, presentations, graphics and databases. It is available for all major operating systems.

This book provides a how-to approach to using Impress, which is Apache OpenOffice.org's presentation application. The book details how to create a presentation and use slide transitions and animations in your presentations.

OpenOffice.org 3.4: Using Impress is the sixth book in Professor Steinberg's *Using Apache OpenOffice.org 3.4* series.

OpenOffice.org 3.4: Using Impress is available in Paperback (ISBN 1492187399) and as a Kindle eBook from your local Amazon website.

OTHER BOOKS BY THE AUTHOR

OpenOffice.org 3.4: Using Draw

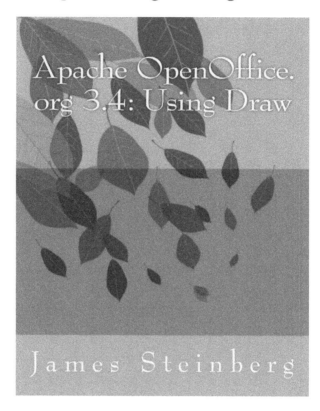

OpenOffice.org is a leading open-source office software suite. It features word processing, spreadsheets, presentations, graphics and databases. It is available for all major operating systems.

This book provides a how-to approach to using Draw, which is Apache OpenOffice.org's vector graphics application. The book details how to create a document comprising of 2D and 3D objects.

OpenOffice.org 3.4: Using Draw is the seventh book in Professor Steinberg's *Using Apache OpenOffice.org 3.4* series.

OpenOffice.org 3.4: Using Impress is available in Paperback (ISBN 1492774065) and as a Kindle eBook from your local Amazon website.

www.ingramcontent.com/pod-product-compliance
Lightning Source LLC
Chambersburg PA
CBHW080420060326
40689CB00019B/4321